I0169311

Northern Shaolin Style

Shaolin #4
Pierce the Heart

Rick L. Wing

Jing Mo Athletic Association
San Francisco, California

First Printing

Copyright © 2017 by Rick L. Wing

All rights reserved. No portion of this book may be reproduced, stored in a retrieval system, or transmitted in any form or by any means – electronic, mechanical, photocopying, recording, scanning, or otherwise – without the prior express written permission of the publisher.

Published by

Jing Mo Association

San Francisco, California

www.jingmo.com

ISBN 0-9771648-4-5

Disclaimer

Please note that the author and publisher of this book are not responsible in any manner whatsoever for any injury that may result from practicing the techniques and/or following the instructions given in this book. Since the physical activities described may be too strenuous in nature to engage in safely, it is essential that a physician be consulted prior to training.

This book is dedicated to
Grandmaster Paul Fung Ngar Tam
Chairman of the Northern Shaolin Gu Ruzhang
Memorial Association in the U.S.A.

The Honored Calligaphy of Grandmaster Paul F. N. Tam

This calligraphy is meant to be read in the traditional manner, from up to down, and right to left. The literal meaning of the words in this poem are as follows,

kung	enter
fu	door
no	leading
style	road
method	need
self	mouth
learning	instruction.

There are many levels of meaning in this poetic couplet. Discuss this with others. Explore and find the deeper levels of meaning. There is the literal meaning, the superficial meaning, and alternatively, other deeper meanings. One should note that the names of three forms, Shaolin #1 #2, and #10, are in the poem. Understanding this poem is a kung fu lesson in itself.

Other alternative renderings of this poem in English are as follows.

When entering the world of kung fu (as a beginner),
you need hands-on, face-to-face teaching.
However, it is up to each individual to achieve and adventure in their own way.

Another interpretation would be the following:

Don't look down on the young people that are just starting to learn kung fu, someday, with self-discipline and hard practice, they too can become a grandmaster on their own.

Note: As with kung fu, there are many levels of understanding to this; some see the superficial meaning, while others will see a deeper meaning. Read, and discover for yourself.

Calligraphy for Rick L. Wing from Grandmaster Paul F. N. Tam

This is respectfully presented to Gin Hing (Rick L. Wing), my younger, close and esteemed martial brother. These words are a gift for you to keep.

健興賢棣惠存

入門領路須口授

功夫無式法自修

譚豐雅題

A novice must be led by verbal instruction, person-to-person, one-on-one. This is the true and traditional way.

Through hard work (kung fu) and self-discipline, one can achieve, and, even transcend the style.

This is written by Tam Fung Ngar (Grandmaster Paul F. N. Tam)

Chinese Proverb and Calligraphy from the late Grandmaster Paul Eng

万　知
夫　柔
之　知
望　剛

Grandmaster Paul Eng
(January 8, 1941 - January 8, 2015)

Among those in the martial world, their fondest hope is to truly understand the interplay between soft and hard.

Editor's note: The literal translation of these characters, from up-to-down and right-to-left, "know soft know hard, million people their hope."

Preface from Rick L. Wing

This book is on Shaolin #4, one of the five short sets of the Northern Shaolin Style. It documents the set as taught to me by Grandmaster Wong Jack Man, but it may also prove of interest to practitioners of other Northern Shaolin lineages. The set varies slightly from instructor to instructor, but is usually more similar than not. This powerful set teaches you how to attack the opponent's centerline using punches and kicks.

And, to my teacher, Grandmaster Wong Jack Man, I pay my greatest respect. Although some say he is a quiet man, a friend of mine said it best when he told me, "When he says a little, he says a lot." How true. I have greatly benefitted in my life from his wise words.

Once upon a time -- looking for advice -- I asked him, "What's the most important thing when a person becomes a sifu?" I assumed he would talk about movement, a technique, a set, a state of mind, or something along those lines, but without any hesitation and with a completely straight face, he replied, "To be a good person." I can not speak as to what he may have told others, I only know that this is what he told me. It told me a lot about what he expected, and it told me a lot about him.

Rick L. Wing
January 28, 2017
Year of the Rooster
San Francisco, California

A young Wong Jack Man waits to catch the straight sword. He is practicing on a rooftop in Hong Kong.

Table of Contents

Lineage Chart

Lineage Chart

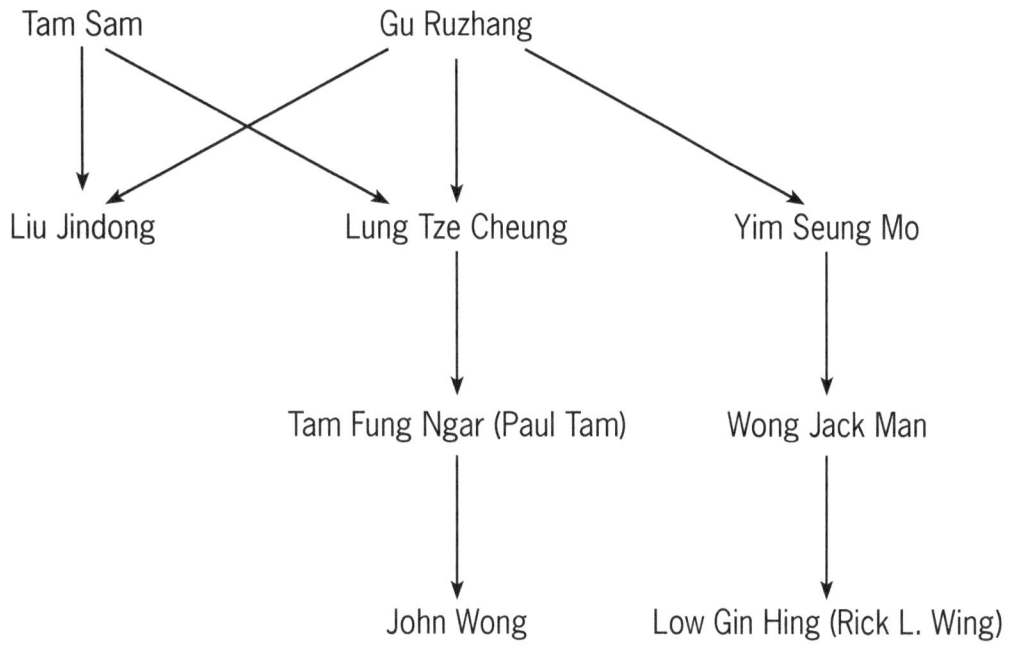

Tam Sam   Gu Ruzhang

Liu Jindong   Lung Tze Cheung   Yim Seung Mo

Tam Fung Ngar (Paul Tam)   Wong Jack Man

John Wong   Low Gin Hing (Rick L. Wing)

Grandmaster Paul Fung Ngar Tam on His Life Experience, Northern Shaolin, and Yijin

By Sifu John Wong and Rick L. Wing

Master Paul F. N. Tam was born on March 26, 1935. He began learning kung fu in Hong Kong in 1948, and became a disciple of Master Lung Tze Cheung, a top student of Gu Ruzhang. Paul advanced rapidly in Master Lung's school, and the Chinese Martial Arts for Health Association appointed him as an Assistant Instructor when he was only sixteen years old. Although very young, many considered him an advanced student and he did most of the teaching for Master Lung at Master Lung's school.

His main emphasis at Lung's school were the Northern Shaolin Style and Yang Style Tai Chi Chuan (as modified by Gu Ruzhang). Some weapons that Paul learned

The author (left), with Master Paul Tam (right).

were Luk Hop Dao (Six Harmony Saber), Lung Ying Gim (Dragon Shape Sword), Tai Lan Cheung (Raise Blocking Spear), Dai Dao (Big Knife), Spring-Autumn Guan Dao, and the Wong Lung Kwun (Yellow Dragon Staff from Choy Lee Fut). He also learned basic level circle walking and the basic hand movements of Ba Gua Zhang.

Since the spear was a very popular military weapon in the Ming and Qing Dynasty, many weapons were used to counter the spear. Paul learned the Single Broadsword versus Spear, Double Broadsword versus Spear, Dai Dao versus Spear, Empty Hands versus Spear, and, even the Bench versus the Spear (from Choy Lee Fut). Lung also taught Paul how to defend himself using a bench, the techniques handed down from Tam Sam. Paul also learned a few hand forms and a bench set from the Buck Sing Choy Lee Fut style.

Though Lung Tze Cheung was one of Gu Ruzhang's top students, he was also encouraged by Gu to learn from Tam Sam, the founder and acknowledged master of the Buck Sing Choy Lee Fut School. Some of Lung's students were taught a few sets of Choy Lee Fut. Lung himself was considered a very high-level Choy Lee Fut master in the Buck Sing Choy Lee Fut lineage.

Paul also learned fighting and sparring techniques from Master Lung. At the time, gloves were not available, so sparring was "controlled" -- as much "control" as one could have since the combatants fought with bare fists and open hands. Injuries were the norm and occurred quite often. From his experience, Paul felt that Choy Lee Fut was more effective for self-defense, but that the Northern Shaolin Style was better for overall health and fitness. Choy Lee Fut has a higher proportion of techniques used for fighting and a lesser proportion for health, but for the Northern Shaolin Style, it is the other way around. However, he also believes that the individual makes the art, and not the other way around.

Master Lung taught Paul on a one-to-one basis, and the relationship between the two was very close. Usually, Master Lung preferred to teach his student two or three at a time, group lessons being easier for the instructor. Since times were hard, Master Lung did not have many students. The war had only recently ended, and many in Hong Kong had to work very hard and had little free time for other activities. Paul found Master Lung to be even-tempered and patient, going over each lesson until the lesson was clear. The Tai Chi that Master Lung taught was the Yang style Tai Chi Chuan that was slightly modified by Gu Ruzhang, so they considered it Gu's Tai Chi Chuan.

Since Master Lung was also a "teet da" doctor, literally an "iron hit" doctor, or bonesetter, he was able to impart this knowledge to Paul. Bone setting was a great supplement to Master Lung's income. Master Lung also stood about five feet seven inches, with Yim Seung Mo being several inches shorter. Paul was about the same height as his teacher, and had a similar build.

Paul also aided in Master Lung's many public demonstrations. During the demonstrations, Master Lung would usually perform weapon sets such as the saber, sword, or spear. One part of the show had Paul putting his head on a table, with one ear on the table and the head turned sideways; a brick then placed on his head. Master Lung would then smash the brick, and his control was so good that he could shatter the brick, without hurting a young Paul.

This type of demonstration was routine, and in all the times it was done, Paul never had any fear that his teacher would hurt him, such was Paul's faith and innate trust in his teacher. Believing in one's sifu was a common characteristic of kung fu students in Hong Kong. Master Lung had the ability to break three stacked bricks.

Paul himself did not learn all of his teacher's iron palm method. He began the practice of iron palm, and although it was a powerful weapon, it did have its downside, so he abandoned the practice very early on. He noted that the practice of iron palm had harmful side effects, even if done correctly. He saw firsthand the severe arthritis that developed in his master's right hand as the master aged. Even then, a young Paul pondered how the martial arts could enhance health without giving rise to adverse effects.

Concerning Gu Ruzhang's famous palm strike on a horse in 1925, Paul mentioned that Master Lung said that he did not actually see Gu Ruzhang kill the horse; he only heard about it later. Lung accompanied Gu Ruzhang and saw him sign a piece of paper, stating that Gu would show up to strike the horse, thus committing himself to appear, and thereby garnering the public's attention towards the upcoming spectacle. Once Gu signed the paper, the advertising for the event could begin in earnest. Even then, media was important and perhaps, a significant factor in what was to become the legend of Gu Ruzhang. Lung subsequently heard that the horse died later, but not immediately in front of the spectators as many believed.

Paul Tam also mentioned that many stories were made up about Gu Ruzhang, but he was only interested in what Gu learned and taught, and not in the many fables and legends which arose concerning the acclaimed iron palm hero. In general, most of what Gu learned was what he learned from Yim Kai Wun before Gu went south. Additionally, it was easier for Gu to make a living teaching northern martial arts to southerners, since his style was common in the north, but rarer in the south. It should also be noted that Gu passed away at a relatively young age, perhaps because he had such a hard life during the war years, or perhaps because of his practice of iron palm, or… possibly both.

Paul learned from Master Lung through 1956. He stopped attending kung fu class due to his having to leave Hong Kong in order to pursue higher education in Taiwan. Subsequently, in 1961, Master Paul Tam graduated from National Taiwan University and returned to Hong Kong to teach Biology, Human Anatomy and Chinese Kung Fu at Catholic Piu-Shing Middle School. This school was one of the top schools in Hong Kong. He taught there for over 28 years. Master Paul Tam also studied acupuncture with the China National Medical School and was granted a lifetime membership in their association. Many of Master Tam's students have doctorates in various fields, some even being doctors of medicine. Master Tam, clearly, is a teacher of teachers.

Looking back, and from his vantage point, Paul believes that the Northern Shaolin Style is good for the creation of a healthy and flexible body. Moves such as the tornado kick teach balance and body control. The kicking methods are useful for health and self-defense. He also believes that a great aid in self-defense is simply having a healthy body, one with the ability to move quickly and with purpose.

In his spare time, Master Tam studied and practiced Wu-Zi Qi Kung, Tai Chi Chuan, and pushing hands under Master Choi Chung Fong. He also practiced Sun Style Tai Chi Chuan under Grandmaster Sun Jian Yun, the daughter of Sun Lu Tang. Paul Tam was named as one of her true disciples. Simply put, Master Tam's martial pedigree is without peer.

Master Tam has been an instructor of a large number of kung fu training courses organized by different industrial and commercial institutions in Hong Kong and the United States. He was appointed secretary, executive and competition adjudicator of the Hong Kong Chinese Martial Arts Association, a post he held for more than ten years. He has contributed immensely to the development of kung fu in Hong Kong. He was elected Chairman of the Northern Shaolin Ku Yu Cheung (Gu Ruzhang) Memorial Association in the United States of America, and many considered him the natural choice for the position.

Master Tam also noted that the current "Jeung Moon" (lineage holder or gateway keeper) of the Northern Shaolin Style in Hong Kong is Sifu Lung Kai Ming, son of Master

Lung Tze Cheung. Wong Jack Man is also listed as being part of this very same lineage.

Under Master Tam's guidance, many of his students act as instructors and judges at various community martial arts tournaments on a regular basis.

Master Paul Tam retired to the United States and he began teaching classes in Yijin in San Jose, California in 2000. In 2005, he founded Tam's Yijin Exercise Institute and he is the lifetime chair of this non-profit organization. His only charitable goal is the betterment of human society. His scientific, logical and systematic approach to human anatomy continues to help many.

Master Tam's genius is that he has used his extensive martial and medical knowledge to create a complete system of exercise for the sole purpose of health and longevity. Some might consider it a form of Chinese yoga, but it is much, much more. Armed with his extensive medical knowledge from both east and west, he has taken the best of the stretching and

This is a group photo of Master Lung's school in Hong Kong. Paul Tam is standing and wearing black trunks and is on the top row, far right, and Master Lung is sitting in the front row, third from the right.
Photo courtesy of Paul Tam.

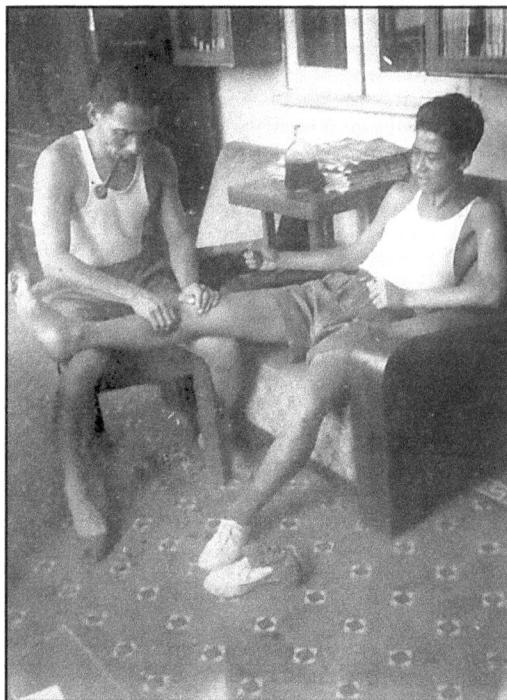

Master Lung smoking his pipe while at the same time massaging and healing Paul's right knee. Notice the bottle of medicinal wine on the table between them.
Photo courtesy of Paul Tam.

moving methods of Northern Shaolin, along with the postures and flow of Tai Chi, to create his own exercise system that is simple yet profound. The adherents of his unique Yijin exercise system have multiplied tenfold, with hundreds, nay, thousands, now attesting to the efficacy of his system. People credit his exercise system with greatly enhancing their health, and his schools have multiplied, with new branches all over the Bay Area, and even one in Hong Kong. Many testimonials are heartfelt and easily given. Many of his students, such as Sifu John Wong, have schools of their own, and they continue to spread the methods of Yijin. This is the legacy of Master Paul Tam.

Master Tam is living proof of his methods. Many admire his flexibility, health, energy, and positive outlook on life. Master Tam's early roots are from the Northern Shaolin Style, but he has since taken a large step forward for humanity with his creation of Yijin, something he continues to share with his large, and ever-increasing, number of students.

These photos are from Lung Tze Cheung's book on the Straight Sword.

In Memory of My Master, Gu Ruzhang

By Song Yuwen

Master Gu Ruzhang

In Memory of My Master, Gu Ruzhang

After our nation has endured two world wars in nearly half a century, many things have been scattered by the wind and have vanished like smoke from a flame. However, my memory of Master Gu is as strong as the memory of my own mother and father. In turn, this reminds me of all my fellow disciples who also learned from Master Gu at the He family ancestral hall located on Wende Road in the city of Guangzhou.

It was my senior fellow apprentice, Long Zixiang, who impressed me the most. He was, in fact, Master Gu's teaching assistant. Although Master Gu certainly demonstrated personally for us at various times, it was this senior fellow apprentice, Long Zixiang, who usually taught us every day.

Gu Ruzhang

My fellow martial apprentices included Lu Wenying, who was considered the fourth of the "Eight Immortals" of the Guangzhou press; Zhong Jiming, a very youthful man who was considered as aggressive as myself in writing and rooting out stories; Luo Xiating, the director of the New Guo Hua Newspaper; Luo Wenxi, the son of Luo Xiating; and Huang Gongjie, who came from Guangxi Province and was in charge of the news agency. Because so many of us were affiliated with the newspaper industry, our group was nicknamed the "journalists" class. After we had finished practicing and the class had ended, we would walk by the Taikang Road and go to the Xianxiang Teahouse on Yonghan South Road to have lunch and drink tea.

Gu Ruzhang demonstrates his strength by lying underneath a heavy stone weighing a thousand pounds. The three students standing on the stone are, from left to right, Long Zixiang, Liu Jindong, and Yan Shangwu.

15

The skills of Master Gu were so high that we could see that he had completely inherited the skill of his ancestors. His grandfather was a famous armed escort in the northern region of China who always displayed three sticks of incense in the caravan as his symbol while he escorted goods at night. Seeing these three incense sticks, the bandits would not dare to rob the caravan and so they nicknamed him, "Three Incenses." Later, his father, Gu Lizhi, inherited the escort company and Gu Lizhi also used three sticks of incense as his symbol, and so, the bandits did not dare to rob any goods from him either. Master Gu carried on the tradition of his forefathers and he became the third generation caravan escort. Because the bandits were suspicious of Master Gu's skills, they decided to test him by attempting to rob his caravan. Unexpectedly, the young third generation master turned out to be quite strong, and he effortlessly drove the bandits away. As a result of this encounter, the nickname, "Three Incenses," won fame and lasted for three full generations, finally ending with Master Gu. This was a story that was told to me about four or five years ago by my senior fellow apprentice, Liu Jindong.

Tan San (Tam Sam in Cantonese), the founder of Buck Sing Choy Lee Fut.

Master Gu's Iron Sand Palm was very well-known in Guangdong Province, so he was constantly being challenged to public duels. A famous boxer named Tan San in Guangzhou then came forward and publicly declared the following, "If anyone wants to fight with Gu Ruzhang, he must fight with me first. If he defeats me, then, and only then, should he even consider himself worthy to fight with Gu Ruzhang." Master Tan San enjoyed a great reputation and was highly respected in the martial world. After Tan San's words, those who challenged Master Gu ceased their arrogant and boastful ways.

Master Tan and Master Gu decided to exchange their students. Our senior fellow apprentice, Long Zixiang was sent to Master Tan as one of the exchange students. Master Tan's student, Liu Jindong, came to learn Iron Sand Palm from Master Gu. Because I worked for the newspaper and had access to a camera and knew how to take good pictures, I was also assigned by Master Gu to take photographs of various moves for Master Tan.

I learned Xingyiquan and Dragon Sword from Master Gu. Around 1936 or 1937, He Jian, the president of the national government in Hunan Province, visited Guangdong Province. Because it was known that He Jian was skilled in the martial arts and because he was known to be a strong advocate of the martial arts, the government of Guangdong Province then held a special martial arts performance at the Guangzhou People's Education

Center in Jing Hui Park on Jing Hui Road. This was done to welcome the honored guest, He Jian. I was scheduled to perform the Dragon Sword, and luckily, even I was able to win a burst of applause from the audience.

On July 7, 1937, China was forced to fight the War of Resistance Against Japan. In November of 1938, Guangzhou fell into enemy hands and Master Gu followed the military school to Deqing County in Guangdong Province since he was the official military trainer and instructor of the school. I also went to the battlefield in the northern region of Guangdong Province as a war correspondent. As a patriot, my fighting was done with pen instead of sword. Although I did not hold any weapons, I wrote many articles about the war in a short period of time.

In the long years that followed, Master Gu, Master Tan, brother Long Zixiang, and brother Liu Jindong have all passed away. I am the only one who is still alive in my class. It fills me with sadness when I reflect on my masters and my brothers of days gone by.

Huang Gongjie, a fellow student in my early "journalists" martial arts class, is the only one I still hate. He was a collaborator and traitor to the Chinese people in Macau and was known as the "King of Murder." This humiliated our teacher and our entire school. I often think that if Master Gu, now in heaven, knew about this, he would smite Huang Gongjie down with one stroke of his Iron Sand Palm.

Early in the morning, September 1, 1983 - Journalists' Day
Song Yuwen

Editor's Note: This was translated from material from the 1st Inaugural Ceremonial Proceedings of the Gu Ruzhang Memorial Association, September 11, 1983, Northern Shaolin Association of Hong Kong. The information was graciously provided by Sifu Paul Fung Ngar Tam of the Northern Shaolin Gu Ruzhang Memorial Association. Sifu Paul F. N. Tam was the former Chairman of the Northern Shaolin Gu Ruzhang Memorial Association in the United States of America.

The Four Basic Weapons of Northern Shaolin

單
刀
棍
槍
劍

單刀

Saber

The saber (or broadsword) is referred to as the "dan dao" or "single knife" in Cantonese. It is one of the most commonly practiced weapons in the kung fu arsenal, and is usually taught first. The saber has a cutting edge that is mainly used for slashing. One may use the tip to thrust with, but its primary strength lies in its strong hacking techniques. The weight of the blade makes for a strong cut and the back of the blade is dull so that one may block or parry with this side. One might also push on the dull side to th rust the blade forward. The pommel may also be used as a bludgeon. Northern sabers are sometimes called "willow leaf" sabers because of the shape of the blade. Most sabers have a groove in the blade so the blood of the opponent will run out along the groove; then the blade will be easier to pull out.

Most people have an instinctual feeling for how they should use the saber. Beginners naturally know how to swing a saber and this makes it a much easier weapon for them to learn first; this is different from the straight sword which is more subtle in its use. They can cut forward with the blade, many times in a "figure-eight" shape. Saber sets emphasize cutting upward, downward, side-to-side, and with various stepping techniques. They are also replete with the requisite spinning and twirling of the weapon. Many times the practitioner will revolve the saber around the body so as to protect one's borders. Although there may be a few kicks in the set, it is the use of the weapon which is preeminent. The empty hand is not often used to strike with, as a saber set will emphasize use of the weapon. Typically, the empty hand is held in the shape of an open palm, and the free arm is used to aid in balance and to add power to the thrust of the saber, either by moving in the opposite direction or the same direction. This depends on how one cuts with the saber. The free hand may also be used to strike and to protect, if need be.

My teacher, Sifu Wong Jack Man, taught the Eight Trigram Broadsword (Bot Gua Dao in Cantonese, Bagua Dao in Mandarin). This set was also one of the ten standard Jing Mo (Jing Wu in

Mandarin) sets taught in the Shanghai curriculum, but, as is usual in Chinese kung fu, there are many variations of this form.

Most weapon sets of a particular style take on the characteristics of that style. If a style emphasizes strength and stability, in general, that will be reflected in that system's weapon forms. As we practiced a northern style, the Eight Trigram Broadsword reflected this, and the set covered a great deal of ground with a great deal of hopping and leaping throughout the form. If one looks carefully, one might also notice that the practitioner moves along the eight directions (north, northwest, west, southwest, south, southeast, east, and northeast). This is shown in the following very simple diagram.

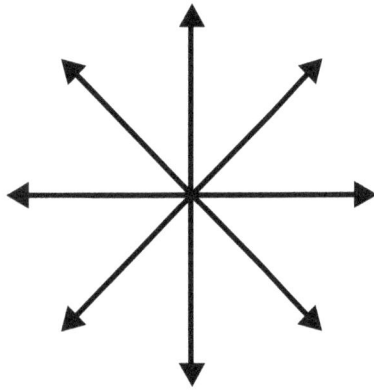

Although the name of this set is Bagua Dao, it is not related to the palm art of Bagua Zhang. It is so named because of the eight directions that the set covers.

The saber should be like a ferocious tiger, slaying all in its path. Sun Yuk Fung (Sun Yufeng in Mandarin) of the Lohan Mun style, was the famous "Broadsword King of Five Provinces," and he used his deadly techniques in his travels as a convoy security chief. Practicing undoubtedly aided in the development of his renowned vice-like grip and his "revolving hands" technique. Fu Zhen Song, famed Dragon Bagua Zhang master, wielded a large and heavy saber in his martial performances. Although he was famous for demonstrating this heavy weapon, it should be noted that the moves of his set were very basic and straightforward. In addition, Fu also demonstrated Bagua techniques with a large stone ball to demonstrate his strength and ability.

Practicing with the saber will increase one's forearm strength, always useful when grabbing or locking an opponent. In our modern day, if a saber is not handy, a stick or rolled-up newspaper might

also prove useful in an emergency. The saber set is a perfect weapon for a beginner to learn first, and one should learn to use this basic weapon to its utmost capability. Doing the set also allows one to practice the required stances and footwork of their style, while learning something new. Shown are a few sequences and poses with the saber so that one may grasp the flavor of this weapon. There are also some basic applications shown to give one the idea of how to use this weapon. Now, go and learn the saber set taught by your own personal instructor.

Saber versus Spear

Block the spear with the back of the blade. Step in, parry the shaft of the spear with the left hand, and then cut.

Saber versus Straight Sword

Parry the sword, step in and slice.

棍

Staff

The staff is the quintessential monk's weapon. Although nondescript and very unthreatening, in the right hands, the staff can be a very dangerous weapon. One can poke with the end, smash with the shaft, clear with the staff… the uses are fairly obvious. Staff forms may be single-ended or double-ended. Although a staff can be used to kill, it would require more effort than say, a dagger, spear, Guan Dao, or any other bladed or sharp weapon. We might even call it "non-lethal" self-defense, as one can easily use a long staff to dissuade someone from attacking, and stopping them *without* causing them serious injury. There is a very famous story where a contingent of Shaolin monks used their iron staffs to literally beat the emperor's enemies into submission.

Staff forms tend to exercise the entire body, and if one does not wish to use it as a weapon, practicing the staff form is excellent exercise for health purposes, as one must put their entire strength into striking with the staff. Practicing with the staff also develops coordination with the entire body. Wielding the staff teaches one to focus power at the end of the staff, if that is what the movement calls for. Many times in the set one will have to slide the hands up and down the shaft (and change grips) to utilize the full potential of the weapon, and this is not something that is easy to do. Be careful, as I have seen many drop the staff inadvertently.

The weapon is a much more dangerous tool when the opponent is not sure how you are coming at him. Imagine the thinking that goes through one's mind when they see someone with a knife coming at them, as the assailant switches the knife from the left hand, to the right hand, to the left hand, and back again. It's a scary prospect. The same can be said of one who uses the staff, and can utilize the staff in any number of ways. The staff, if utilized in many different ways, can bewilder one's opponent.

Although some styles utilize one basic grip on the staff, northern staff sets tend to change their grip on the staff quite often, exploiting the versatility of the weapon. Although working with the staff will increase the power of the grip, it is more useful in developing the strength of the shoulders and the back. Using a very heavy staff will undoubtedly increase one's strength even more. The typical grip that one uses for a northern staff form is to hold the staff with the right hand forward and the left hand held further back on the shaft. The right hand is used to generate the power to strike downward with the forward end.

The set I learned from my teacher was called "Da Sot Kwun" in Cantonese. This set was from my teacher's Ma Kin Fung lineage. The words literally mean "ground hell/underworld staff." It was a reference to this demon or god who came from the underworld, and this meant that the set was to be done with the fury of a wrathful demon god. Our set was a very long one, and was as much a memory exercise as it was exercise for the body. It was arduous (or should I say "exhilarating?") both mentally and physically. The only movement that my teacher ever mentioned as having a name was something about the roots of a tree going underground, or perhaps poking out from the soil.

I did notice that when I saw people practice this set, upon completion of the set, the first thing that most people would do would be to put the staff down, as if to say, "I'm done with this." Come to think of it, most people would do that upon completing any weapon set, especially with the saber or double sabers; however with the straight sword, I would say not so much. People would put the saber down quickly because it would be their right forearm that got tired and sore; with the staff, people would put it down because their whole body was fatigued.

Doing this set required that one have good stamina, and a very high sense of manual dexterity. Out of the four basic weapons, the staff set was clearly the one that stood out in terms of over-all body exercise. Although one could catalog the many different ways that one could use a staff in self-defense, it would probably be easier to simply learn a very complicated staff set such as the one that was taught by our teacher, Sifu Wong Jack Man. Even

now, many years after I learned his staff form, one which we both agreed was one of the very best that we have ever seen, I still enjoy going through all the moves, and I wonder at the remarkable level of thought that it took to create such a set as this.

May you learn such a set from your own instructor, and explore the staff set that you know and see all the applications that it has to offer.

Staff versus Spear - sequence 1

Parry his spear thrust by moving the staff back and up, then strike down.

Staff versus Spear - sequence 2

Parry his strike to the left and then poke him hard in the chest.

捨

Spear

The spear by its very nature is a lethal weapon. It is basically a dagger attached to a long pole. If directed at the proper target, one thrust of the spear can kill or wound. It is a pinpoint weapon, and although the tip is the most lethal part of the spear, the shaft and butt end of the spear can also be used, either offensively or defensively.

The focal point of any spear set is obviously the tip, and practicing with the spear teaches one to focus their own energy at the small point. Although spear sets will have twirling and spinning moves, its true lethality comes from spearing directly forward with the spear tip.

It is no wonder that in times where guns were not prevalent, it was the spear that was known as the "King of Weapons." Even before the advent of "hot arms" i.e. muskets, pistols, and guns of any sort, the spear was still the king of weapons during the hey-day of "cold-arms" i.e. swords, spears, etc.

Gu Ruzhang, the famous iron-palm master, was known as the "God of Spear," and during his years as a convoy guard, this was his chosen weapon. Gu was known for performing his "Raise Blocking Spear" set. Whether Gu developed this set himself or learned it from someone else is not known. All we know is that he did learn his martial art from Yim Kai Wun, known as "Great Spear Yim." Fu Zhensong, another one of the "Five Northern Tigers," also used an iron spear for purposes of self-defense. It is well-known in martial history that Fu Zhensong used his iron spear to fight off a large gang of bandits, and also dueled with the top spearmen of his day, one such being Li Shuwen, a famous Baji fighter and teacher. Fu's famous spear set was known as the "Four-Faced Spear." It might also be translated as the "Four-Sided Spear."

In addition to teaching the "Raise Blocking Spar," this set coming from the lineage of Yim Kai Wun, to Gu Ruzhang, to Yim Seung Mo, and down to Wong Jack Man, my teacher also taught the Plum

Blossom Spear, from Ma Kin Fung. "Raise Blocking Spear" is a medium length set and it emphasizes the basic spear technique of block, press, and thrust. There are spinning techniques, clearing techniques, cutting techniques, and even a move where one withdraws the spear behind the head, only to then shoot if forward.

In contrast to the "Raise Blocking Spear," the Plum Blossom Spear was a much more flowery set with spinning the spear around the waist and over the head, and holding the spear and using it as one might use a staff. The surprise move of this set was to shoot the spear underneath and between the legs to shoot out in the opposite direction. This set also utilized the grip of the left hand held behind and the right hand in front, uncommon for a northern spear set. Both sets required a great deal of coordination, and one had to be careful not to let the spear slip out of one's hands. The idea is that if one has the ability to make the spear go through all these motions, one should easily have the ability to use the spear for a more direct and simple purpose, to thrust at the opponent to cause him injury.

Typically, northern spear sets are done with the left hand held forward and the right hand held in the back, thus using the more powerful arm to drive the spear forward. Most southern spear sets, perhaps influenced and developed from northern staff sets, place the right arm forward and the left hand is held in the back. Although the spear tip is obviously the "center point" of the set, watch how your spear set uses the butt end, and the shaft, to either attack or defend. Also, watch to see if you spear set has any surprise maneuvers in it.

Spear continued on next page.

Spear Thrusting - sequence 1

This is the most basic move of the spear. Raise up the back of the spear to block, bring it down, and then thrust the spear forward.

Spear Thrusting - sequence 2

Bring the spear behind the head, then shoot it forward. Step forward with the right leg and push the spear even further forward.

Spear versus Guan Dao - sequence 1

Lift the left leg to avoid the cut of the Guan Dao. After the blade has swung past, spear him in the side.

Spear versus Guan Dao - sequence 2

As before, avoid the cut of the Guan Dao. Then, step in and strike using the butt end of the spear. Counter the heft of the Guan Dao with the speed of the spear.

劍

Straight Sword

The straight sword (gim in Cantonese, jian in Mandarin) is an elegant weapon. The blade is sharp on all sides, and the tip and the blade near the tip are the main striking and cutting areas. Unlike the saber, the sword is a finesse weapon, and one must be agile and evasive. The blade is not meant to be used for hacking. The blade can be used for parrying and blocking if need be. When wielding the straight sword, one should use pinpoint control and go for the vital points. Many of the sword thrusts are to be directed at the opponent's wrist, thus disabling him and disconnecting him from his weapon. One of the most significant differences between the straight sword and the saber is that because the straight sword has a sharpened tip, there are many more straight thrusts as opposed to the cutting and slashing techniques of the saber.

The open hand, when not poking or striking pressure points, is usually held in the "sword fingers" position. Holding the free hand in this way should accentuate the stabs, pokes, and cuts of the sword, either by moving in the same direction as the sword or acting as a counterbalance to the movement of the sword. One might even get a sense of a practitioner's skill with the sword by observing how he or she uses this free hand. Keep this in mind when you are learning the movements of the sword.

One of Yim Seung Mo's favorite sets was Da Mo Gim, a slow, flowing sword set. When doing this weapon, one typically gives it the flavor of the Tai Chi Sword. It is also said that Sun Lutang's favorite weapon was the straight sword. Even scholars would wear swords as decoration during the Ming Dynasty, and many considered it a gentlemen's weapon.

The most famous sword player in China was said to be Li Jinglin (Lee Ging Lum in Cantonese), also known as "Magic Sword Li." He shared his Wudang sword method with many famous martial artists of his time, including Gu Ruzhang. However, so impressed was Li Jinglin with the art of Tai Chi

that he subsequently learned Yang Style Tai Chi from Yang Jianhou, and it was from Li whom Gu Ruzhang learned Tai Chi. The straight sword was also favored by Sun Lutang, another contemporary of Gu. Sun preferred the subtlety of the straight sword and liked the fact the straight sword, in addition to the tip, was sharp on both sides.

As was typical of many of the sets that Wong Jack Man taught, the sword form was also very lengthy. He taught the "Dragon-Phoenix Sword" form (Lung Fung Gim). This set, like many others of its type, utilizes all parts of the sword, the tip, the blade, the pommel, and in many and various ways. Since it was a northern set, there were also many kicks in the set, and much spinning of the sword (and of the body). The set was noted for its one-legged knee bend near the end of the set, something that most people, I should add, did not enjoy doing. Although the set does emphasize the straight thrust, there is also much parrying, blocking, and slashing with the sword, all at various angles and levels. Sifu Wong Jack Man also taught a sword versus sword sparring set, and the set was called "Six Combinations" or "Luk Hop Gim." This set mainly emphasizes evasion and counterattack and does not seek to match force with force.

The sword should seem as a lady dancing, moving from side to side, forward and backward with grace and fluidity. Sheer power is not required; the mind too must be sharp and alert. Someone using a saber forces their opponent to move because of their vigorous attack. When one uses the straight sword, one is looking to exploit the opponent's weak points, and is ready to exploit any opening immediately. When practicing with the sword, one must fuse mind and body together in a coordinated whole. Yin and yang must ebb and flow as one does this set. Although the use of the sword is softer than the saber, it is just as deadly. Tactics, rather than sheer power, is paramount.

It is said that it takes 100 days to wield a saber properly, 1,000 days to master the spear, but 10,000 days to master the sword!

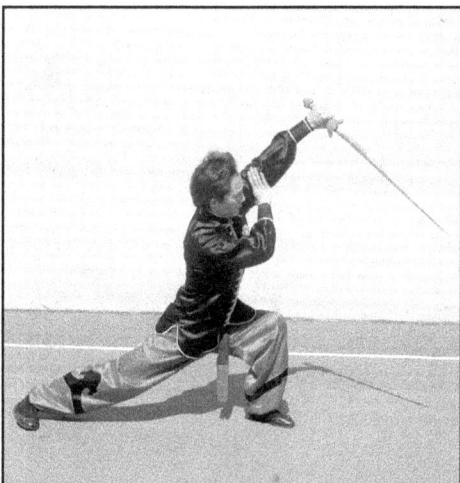

Straight Sword continued on next page.

Straight Sword versus Guan Dao

Avoid the blade of the Guan Dao and cut his leading hand.

Straight Sword versus Saber

Draw him out by threatening him with a straight thrust. Then, withdraw, and thrust again. In other words, threaten him, and after his block goes by, stab him.

Commentary on Shaolin #4

Commentary on Shaolin #4

Shaolin #4 is called "Chuen Sum" in Cantonese, or "Chuan Xin" in Mandarin. These words translate to "pierce the heart" or "to go through the heart." We might also call this set, "Piercing the Heart." This means, some say, that many of the techniques in this set are designed to attack the opponent by striking at his chest. In other words, many of the strikes in this set are considered mid-level attacks. On the other hand, other practitioners might say that the set is named for only one particular signature movement in the set, one that clearly resembles the act of "piercing the heart." It should be noted that most of the techniques in the ten Northern Shaolin Style forms also strike at chest level. This is a point of debate, even among advanced practitioners. After practicing this set and examining it thoroughly, the point of view you wish to take is clearly yours.

This set is usually taught after the practitioner has learned the two beginning sets, Shaolin #6 (Close Strike) and Shaolin #7 (Plum Blossom). After these first two sets are taught, a practitioner may learn Shaolin #4, #5, or #8 next, depending on the decision of your instructor or the usual order of the curriculum of your school.

When I first learned this form, I did not find it to be particularly hard, as many of the moves were at the same level of difficulty as those in Shaolin #6 and #7.

The signature move of this form is movement #2, which is a strong uppercut that is directed skyward. This move occurs three times in the set and would be the single move that seems to define the set. This powerful fist strike may be aimed directly beneath the opponent's chin, or it may be directed at his chest, thus the name "Pierce the Heart." This movement follows a typical sequence in the Northern Shaolin forms of clear, clear and then strike. Oddly, the name of this particular movement in the traditional lyrics is *not* "Pierce the Heart."

The other powerful technique, in this case a foot technique, is that of movement #9A. This kick, a front heel kick, is nicknamed "chuen sum tui" in Cantonese, or "pierce the heart" kick. The idea is that one develops a kick so powerful that it would be able to knock the opponent down with one blow. Of course, most of us only wish it were so. This takes serious practice and repetition. Although my instructor called this technique the "pierce the heart" kick, it is not so named in the lyrics. Perhaps this is just one of those things that a teacher passes verbally to his students.

Although these movements may seem mundane and basic, it should be said that the most effective techniques are basic techniques used correctly at the proper time. Although Shaolin #4 is not extremely flashy, it is still a very useful set if the set is examined thoroughly for its self-defense techniques.

Let me mention some of the other techniques that are unique to this set. Movements #8A and #8B, which consist of a right-handed downward thrust punch followed by a left uppercut, is a sequence that appears solely in Shaolin #4. This teaches a practitioner to attack the upper level of the opponent, and then to attack the lower level.

The next move, that of a front heel kick followed by a side kick with the same leg, is the only time in the five short forms of the Northern Shaolin Style that there are two high kicks done with the same leg without putting the foot down. For this reason, some instructors might teach this set third in the series.

This set, if we restrict ourselves to discussing the first five short forms, also introduces the standing lotus kick, a circular kick designed to strike at the upper torso of the opponent. This movement is followed by simultaneous left and right fist strikes directed at the chest. For the reader, again, please examine this set carefully for the moves directed against the upper torso of the opponent and dwell on this. See if you can make sense of what the ancients were attempting to teach us by offering us these moves.

Movements #14 and #15 work very well in combination. These moves teach one to attack an opponent at mid-level with a right-handed fist strike first directed at the stomach or chest, then follow with a left-handed clearing motion, and finally coming over the top to strike at the opponent's head. "Vicious tiger comes out of the cave" is a beautiful name for the intent and ferocity which the practitioner should emulate, all, of course, in the name of self-defense.

Another move seen in this form which is not in the other five short forms but is seen in the longer forms of Shaolin #1 and Shaolin #10 is movement #18. In this move, the practitioner jumps up and slaps both palms together and then comes down to the ground. This move signifies the striking of the opponent's ears in a forceful manner, and the name "strike the bell" … well, I am sure the reader can figure this out.

Although this set has a tornado kick and double kicks, notice that there is a new hand motion for the flying kick in movement #19. Preceding this particular flying kick, the practitioner should make continuous circular upward motions with the arms, thus clearing the way by knocking the opponent's arms upward. In the regular double flying kick of movement #39, the practitioner blocks downward before executing the kick. Please keep these hand motions in mind when practicing the set because although some kicks may appear to be the same, there are in fact significant differences. One might also think of this kick as a double flying kick using the heel or the side of the foot, instead of the toe or instep, as the contact point.

I would also like to mention movement #37B. Many practitioners may have seen the common hand motion known as "dancing with the flowers," as this hand motion appears throughout the ten forms of the Northern Shaolin Style, and is introduced in Shaolin #6. Typically, this motion ends with a left hooked hand and a right palm, but in this one instance, the motion ends with a right hooked hand and a left palm. The practitioner should understand that a characteristic of the Northern Shaolin Style is that typically, throughout the sets in the system, one side of the body is usually favored over the other. To be good at doing techniques on both sides, the practitioner must practice certain techniques outside of the confines of the form. For example, if a practitioner is learning the Northern Shaolin Style, he will notice that many of the straightforward double kicks are done with the right leg. How many of the straightforward double kicks are done with the left leg? The answer is… none. If one wants to be good at double kicks using the left leg, one would have to practice that kick by itself.

Techniques in Shaolin #4 that are also common in the other sets of the system are the typical right leg heel kicks, along with the double fist strikes, or the strong right-handed fist strike, and the sweep. Once a practitioner begins learning the Northern Shaolin System, he will be able to see techniques which are common among all the sets, and techniques which only occur in one or two of the forms.

What else can be said for the set "Pierce the Heart?" or Shaolin #4? Most of the techniques are straightforward and there are not many complex twisting or turning maneuvers. It is not especially difficult to memorize the moves in this form as many are repeated. There is also a large section of the form that is repeated. Shaolin #4 flows exceptionally well, with most of the power emanating from the upper torso. It is a good workout, especially for the shoulders and chest. Use a light, strong strength throughout the set and feel the flow of the movements. This is what the ancients have passed down to you. And I don't mean me, I mean the people much before me… but I'm getting there, as everyone seems to tell me. I also note that when it comes to getting old… there aren't too many alternatives.

Shaolin #4: Pierce the Heart - The Form

四路少林拳

穿心

第四路 穿心少林拳

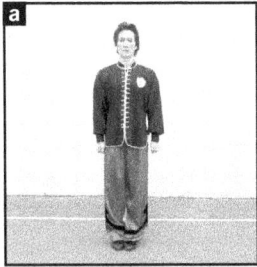

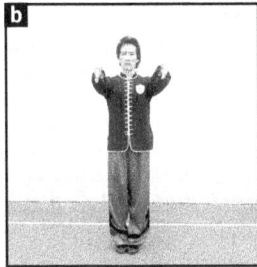

Salute.

The Salute: Stand at attention with fists at your sides. In one continuous motion, raise your hands all the way up, and then push down with both palms. Turn the fingertips slightly inward. This is the Northern Shaolin salute.

一、 仙 人 彈 衣

1A - Immortal shakes his clothes (left).

Step out and to the left with the left leg and trace a counter-clockwise circular shape on the floor. Momentarily, the weight will be on the left leg.

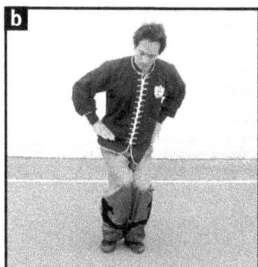

一、上步

1B - Immortal shakes his clothes (right). Step Forward.

Now, with the right foot, trace a clockwise circular shape on the floor by first bringing the right foot alongside the left foot and then forward and to the right. Do this in one continuous motion.

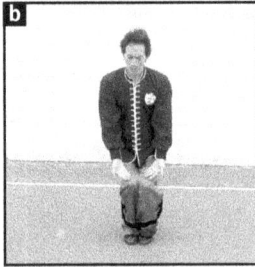

一、雙對拳

1C - Double matching fists.

As you bring the left foot alongside the right foot, bring your hands forward, palms up, and bend your knees slightly.

As you dip down and bend your knees slightly, brush the backs of both hands against the top of your thighs.

Next, bring both hands forward in a circular motion forming fists with both hands. Bring both hands forward as you stand up with your legs straight. Your hands should be held at approximately chest level when completing this movement.

Continued on next page.

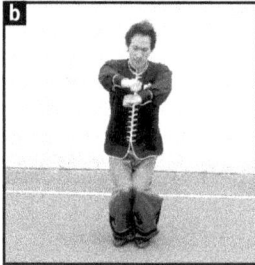

二、舞花七星冲天炮左丁式

2 - (Hands) Dancing with the flowers.
Seven Stars.

As you cross your right arm over your left, the right fist moving from right to left and the left fist moving from left to right, stamp the right foot on the ground and step out in a stance that places most of the weight on the right leg. Some practitioners will sit in a left cat stance while others will open the stance more and place the left foot farther from the right foot so they sit with more stability. Either method is acceptable.

二、 舞 花 七 星 冲 天 炮 左 丁 式

2 continued -
Shoot up to the sky like a cannon (uppercut).
Left cat stance.

As the right forearm arm crosses over
the left forearm, the right fist will continue its
large clockwise circular motion, ending with
the right fist striking straight up. The left fist
will reverse direction, drop down, and then
make a clockwise circular motion with the
left fist dropping down as the right fist shoots
up inside the left arm. The left fist ends in a
position below the right elbow. It should be
clear why this movement is named "Shoot
up to the sky like a cannon (uppercut)." This
movement appears twice more in the form.

三、英雄獨立提左足

3 -   Hero stands on one leg. Pick up the left foot.

Lift the left leg into a crane stance. Then kick out with a left leg toe kick at a 45-degree angle to the left side. After completing the kick, place the left foot back on the ground.

Note: My instructor did not teach me this particular movement in the set, and some may do this move simply as a knee raise instead of a left leg toe kick. This movement is optional and I include it solely because it was in the lyrics for Shaolin #4. When practicing this set, you may go immediately from movement #2 to movement #4 if you like. Either of the different ways are acceptable.

Also, notice that later in the set, the cannon (uppercut) strike is followed by a high left leg kick.

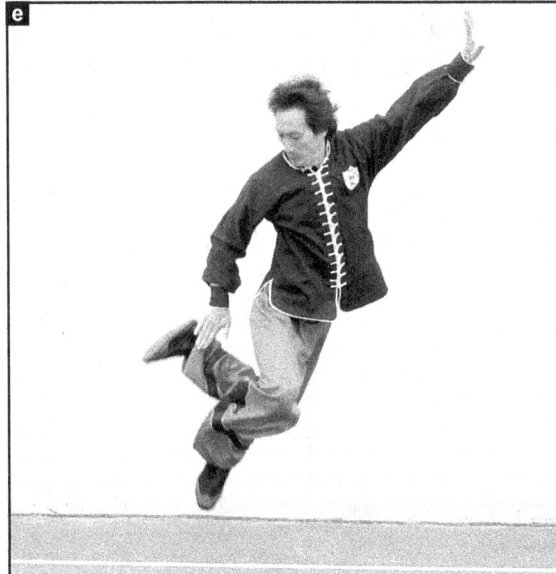

四、後盤腿

4 - Rear coiling kick.

Shift the weight onto the left leg and raise the right leg off of the ground. Then, push off with the left leg and slap the inside of the left ankle with the palm of the right hand. The left hand will rise up naturally. Some practitioners jump in place, and some jump to the left and attempt to cover ground. Some will try and make this left foot back kick high, while others will do the kick lower to the ground but more quickly. Either way is acceptable.

五、摟手衝拳右

5A - Pulling hand (left). Straight thrust punch (right).

As you slap the left foot with the right hand, the right foot falls to the ground.

As you place your left foot on the ground and shift into a left bow stance, make a counter-clockwise clearing motion with an open left hand and strike with a right vertical fist. The left hand becomes a fist and moves to the left side of your body.

back view

五、十字腿左拳

5B - Right "cross" kick or Right "ten" character kick with a left thrusting punch.

Kick forward with the right heel and punch forward with a left vertical fist.

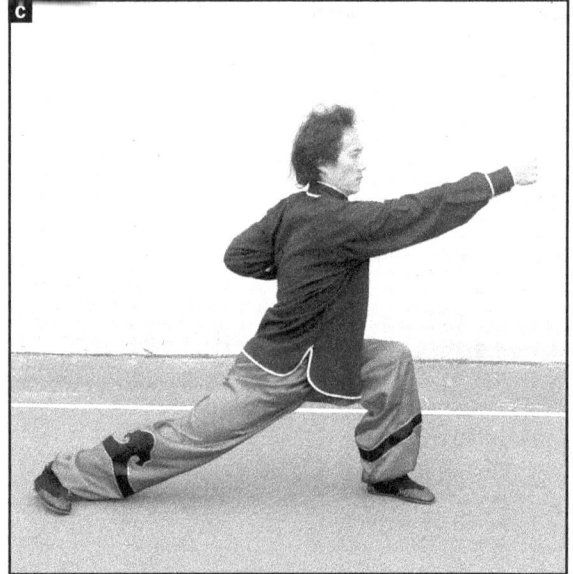

五、拳右

5C - Right thrusting punch. Left bow stance.

Then, while withdrawing your right leg to sit in a left bow stance, punch forward with a right vertical fist as the left hand withdraws to the left side of the body.

六. 左右衝拳坐馬式

6 - Left, right thrusting punches. Sit on horse stance

Turn your torso slightly to your right and shift into a horse stance. As you sit down in your horse stance, withdraw both left and right fists to shoulder level, then punch out simultaneously to both sides of your body. Look to your right side.

七， 迎 面

7A - Approach the Face.

Step your left leg past the right leg so that you sit in a right T-stance. The left leg will step behind the right leg as it moves to the right T-stance. Turn your body to the left and bring the right arm down to the left arm so that the outside of the right forearm rests against the inside of the left forearm. Both hands are now open. The blade edges of both palms face downward, and the palms of both hands face outward.

七． 舞 花 倒 退 步

7B - Hands dancing with the flowers. Step back.

While stepping back with the right leg into a left cat stance, both hands begin to make a large clockwise motion. At the outset, the right hand will go up and the left hand will move down. Both hands continue their circular motion. The right palm moves upward past the bicep of the left arm while the left hand hooks downward. Finally, the right palm faces outward and the left hand ends in the crane's beak position.

side view

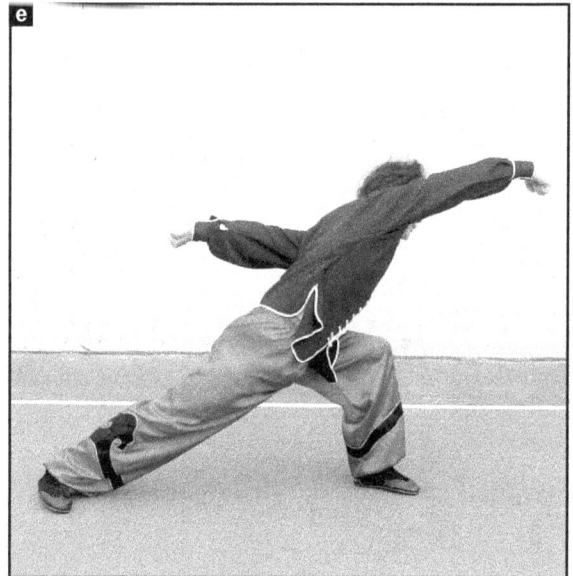

八、 插 拳 炮 拳

8A - Hammering downward thrust punch.

As the left foot steps out into a left bow stance, make a large counter-clockwise motion with the left arm, first down and backward, then upward and finally downward, as you grab with the left hand and punch downward in a counter-clockwise arc with a right horizontal fist. The right hand follows the left hand.

back view

70

八、 海 底 撈 月

8B - Scoop the moon's reflection from the bottom of the sea.

As you rise up and turn your body to the right so that you sit in a horse stance, block upward with the right arm and make an uppercut punch with the left fist.

As an option, some practitioners will open their left hand and make a grabbing motion, finally ending with the fingers closing so that the final position of the left hand is the same. This is not shown in the photos.

九, 左摟右衝拳前

9A - Left hand presses down, right thrust punch. Front heel kick

Turn the left fist so that the palm faces down and the left arm is across the chest. As the left arm blocks downward, strike with a right vertical fist over the left arm, and kick forward and upward with the right heel.

Kick as high as is comfortable for you. You may practice for exercise, application, or both. The choice is yours.

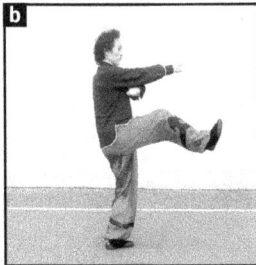

九. 蹬足後踢足

9B - Back heel kick.

Turn to your right, and swing the right leg back in the opposite direction so that you do a right side kick. As the right leg kicks out, the right hand will move to the "guard" position near the left armpit as the left palm pushes backward. Be careful to maintain your balance. If you have a tendency to wobble while doing this move, simply kick lower. You may raise your kick over time if the move is not easy for you. Perseverance is key to obtaining true skill.

九. 反身直立式

9C - Turn around. "Standing up straight" posture.

Place your right foot on the ground and turn your body to the right. The right hand moves in a clockwise clearing motion, followed by the same motion of the left hand. As the left foot steps past the right foot, stand up straight, and the left hand will finally hook upward as the right hand moves to the "guard" position. You may look to the left side as you complete the move. Then, look to your right in anticipation of the next move.

back view

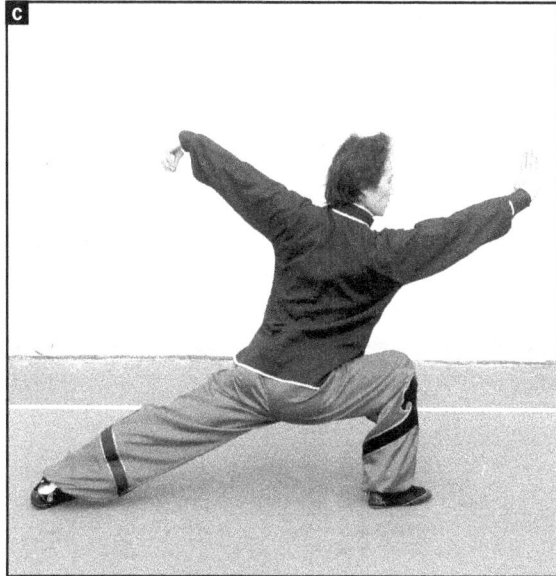

十、 懶 龍 伸 腰 蹬 弓 式

10 - Lazy dragon stretches his back.
Right bow stance

Step out with the right leg into a right bow stance. As the right leg is stepping out, the right hand will move in a circular motion, down and then up, as you flash the right palm.

back view

十一. 偷 步 擺 蓮

11A - Steal a step.
(Right) Lotus kick.

The left foot then steps from behind, and past the right foot, so that you sit in a right T-stance. Then, slap the instep of the right foot with the left palm and right palm in succession, as you do a right leg lotus kick (outward crescent kick). When you slap your right foot, the fingertips of each hand point toward the right.

back view

十一、 十 字 拳

11B - "Ten" character fist.

As you put your right foot down and shift into a right bow stance, the arms cross over each other, right arm moving from right to left and the left arm moving from left to right. This is another "pierce the heart" movement. As your hands continue their movement inward, the lower part of the right forearm will brush the top of the left forearm, and the arms will make an "X" pattern. Then, raise both fists up so that they are at shoulder level and punch outward with both fists. Look in the direction of your left fist. When both hands strike outward, this also "pierces the heart."

side view

十二. 舞花七星沖天炮左丁式

12 - (Hands) Dancing with the flowers.
Seven stars.
Shoot up to the sky like a cannon (uppercut).
Left cat stance.

Swing the right arm over to the left so that the right forearm crosses over the left forearm and stamp the ground with the right foot. This begins the same motion as previously described as "Shoot up to the sky like a cannon (uppercut)."

back view

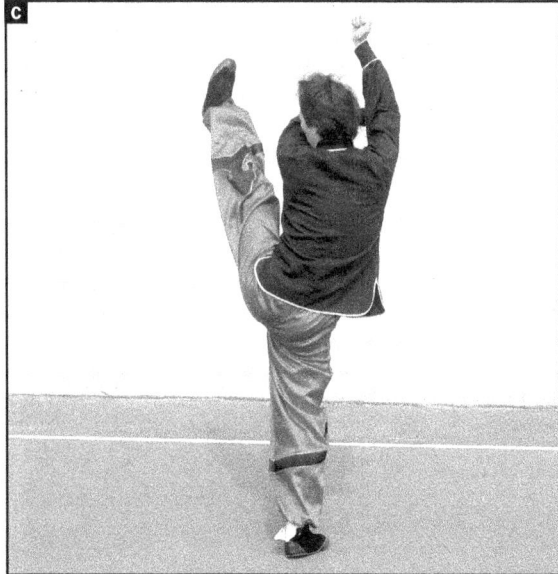

十三、 英 雄 獨 立

13 - Hero's single leg stance. Left leg kick.

Lift the left leg into a crane stance. Then kick out with a left leg toe kick at a 45-degree angle to the left side. Kicking high or low is a matter of choice. Also, some practitioners emphasize height when doing this kick, while others will emphasize penetration. Either way is acceptable.

back view

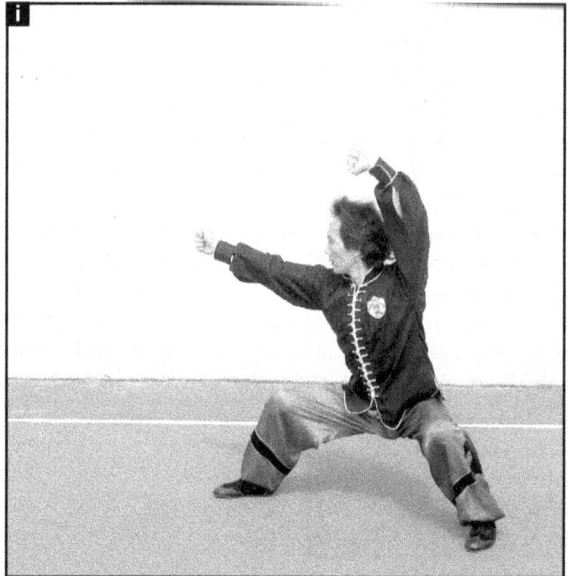

十四. 猛虎出洞坐馬架打式

14 - Vicious tiger comes out of the cave.
Sit on horse stance.
Block and strike.

Place the left foot on the ground, and then push off with the left foot as the right leg slides past the left so that you sit in a horse stance. As you are moving into the horse stance, the left hand blocks upward in a rising counter-clockwise motion as you strike with a right vertical fist. Your horse stance is at a 45-degree angle off the centerline.

十五. 合 步 連 環 拳

15 - "Bring the feet together" stance.
Continuous punch.

As you bring the left foot alongside the right foot, the left fist moves forward in a clockwise downward block as the right vertical fist comes out to strike in a rising clockwise arc. The right fist brushes past the inside of the left elbow as it comes out to strike. Imagine that you are striking your opponent at face level.

十六、穿心舞花十字拳

16 - Pierce the heart. (Hands) dancing with the flowers. "Ten" character fist.

Turn to your left and step your right foot past the front of the left foot so that you temporarily sit in a right T-stance. Bring your right arm over and down and cross both arms in front of you in an "X" position, so that the right arm is on the outside. This is the literal "Pierce the Heart" movement.

Then, step forward with the left leg into a left bow stance and raise both fists to shoulder level. Strike outward with both arms. Look to your left.

side view

十七、坐馬打虎式

17A - Sit on horse stance. Strike the tiger (right).

Turn your waist very slightly to the right so that you temporarily sit in a horse stance. Then make a downward sideways block with the left outer forearm, and strike with your right forearm (or fist). Simultaneously, shift into the left bow stance.

十七、坐馬打虎式

17B - Sit on horse stance. Strike the tiger (left).

Next, make a right downward block and strike with the left outer forearm (or fist). Shift into a right bow stance.

十七、坐馬打虎式

17C - Sit on horse stance. Strike the tiger posture.

Finally, to complete the "Strike the tiger" posture, move the left hand in a clockwise circle and raise your right arm up. As your arms cross, the right arm is on the outside. Sit in a horse stance.

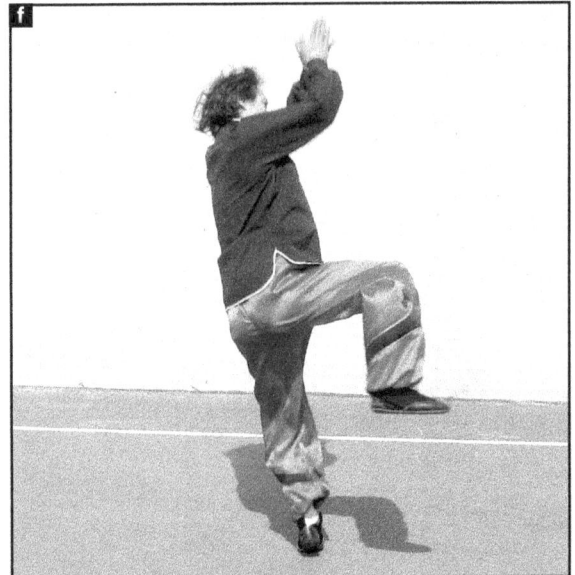

十八. 鐘鼓齊鳴

18A - Strike the bell and hit the drum. (Alternate name: Double wind strikes the ears).

Shift all of your weight onto your right leg, lift the left leg off of the ground, and then push off with the right leg. When you are in the air, turn your body to the left, raise both hands up, and clap the palms together as you are coming down to the ground.

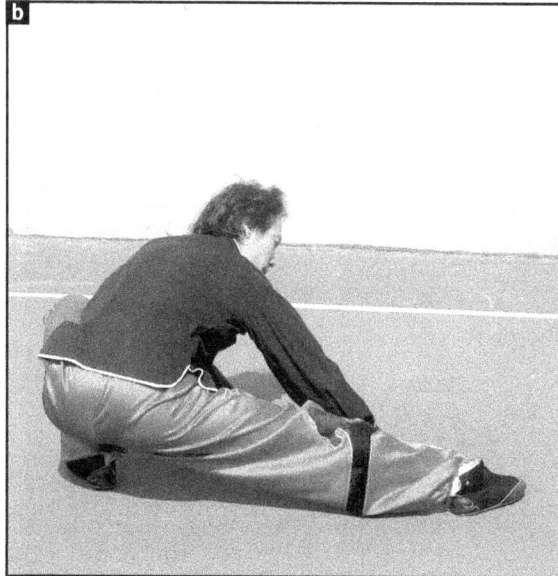

十八．落地伏虎式

18B - Come down to the ground. "Tame the tiger" stance.

As you land in a right scattered stance, slap the ground with both hands. Movements 18A and 18B should be executed in one seamless motion.

back view

十九、上步

19A - Step forward.

Next, raise your body up and shift your weight onto the right leg as you block upward in a large counter-clockwise circular motion with the left hand. As you step forward with the left leg, the right hand will block forward and upward in a large clockwise circular motion. Take several steps, coordinating the circular blocking motion of the hands with the movement of the feet.

十九、掛面腿

19B - Swinging kick to the face.

Finally, as you swing the left leg up and then the right leg to complete the kick, slap the inside of the right foot with the left palm. Jump up and kick as high as you can. Of course, however much effort you would like to put into the set is at your discretion.

side/back view

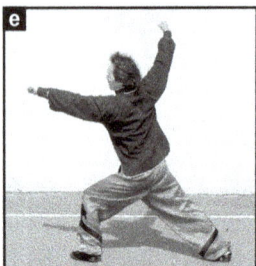

二十、 插拳 炮拳

20A - Hammering downward thrust punch.

Because of the body's forward momentum, you will land with the right leg forward. After the right leg lands, turn in the opposite direction and grab with the left hand and strike with the right hand as you shift into a left bow stance. This next sequence will bring us to the same sequence as shown previously in movement #8. The next sequence of movements from movement #20 to movement #29 will be exactly the same as the sequence of movements shown in movements #8 to #17.

二十、回身海底撈月

20B - Scoop the moon's reflection from the bottom of the sea.

Now, as you rise up and turn your body to the right so that you sit in a horse stance, block upward with the right arm (the outside of the right forearm faces upward) and throw an uppercut punch with the left fist.

二一、左摟右衝拳前

21A - Left hand presses down, right thrust punch. Front heel kick.

Turn the left fist so that the palm faces down and the left arm is across the chest. As the left arm blocks downward, strike with a right vertical fist over the left arm, and kick forward and upward with the right heel.

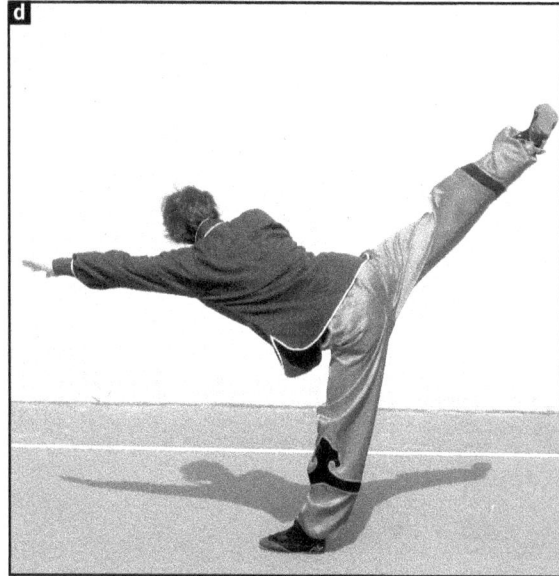

二一、 蹬足後蹬足

21B - Back heel kick.

Turn to your right, and swing the right leg back in the opposite direction so that you do a right side kick. As the right leg kicks out, the right hand will move to the "guard" position as the left palm pushes backward. Maintain your balance.

二一、 反身直立式

21C - Turn around. "Standing up straight" posture.

Place your right foot on the ground and turn your body to the right. The right hand will move in a clockwise clearing motion, followed by the same motion of the left hand. As the left foot steps past the right foot, stand up straight, and the left hand will hook upward as the right hand moves to the "guard" position. Look to your left side.

二二. 懶龍伸腰蹬弓式

22 - Lazy dragon stretches his back.
Right bow stance.

Step out with the right leg into a right bow stance. As the right leg is stepping out, the right hand will move in a circular motion, down and then up, as you flash the right palm.

二三、偷步擺連

23A - Steal a step.
(Right) Lotus kick.

The left foot will step from behind, and past the right foot, so that you temporarily sit in a right T-stance. Then slap the instep of the right foot with the left palm and right palm in succession, as you do a right leg lotus kick (outward crescent kick).

二三、十字拳

23B - "Ten" character fist.

As you put your right foot down and shift into a right bow stance, the arms cross over each other, the right arm moving from right to left and the left arm moving from left to right. The lower part of the right forearm will brush the top of the left forearm, and the arms make an "X" pattern. Then raise both fists up so that they are at shoulder level and then punch outward with both fists. Look in the direction of your left fist.

Notice that these are the same movements as previously done in movement #16; only the name is abbreviated.

二四. 舞花 七星 冲天炮左丁式

24 - (Hands) Dancing with the flowers.
Seven stars.
Shoot up to the sky like a cannon (uppercut).
Left cat stance.

Swing the right arm over to the left so that the right forearm crosses over the left forearm and stamp the ground with the right foot. This begins the same motion as previously described as "Shoot up to the sky like a cannon (uppercut)."

98

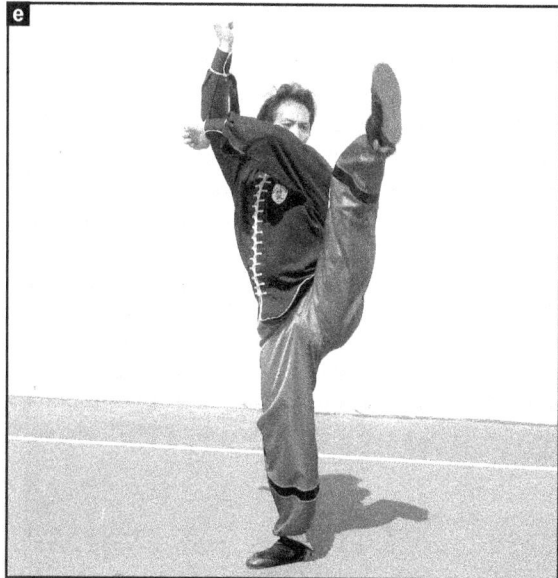

二五、 英 雄 獨 立

25 - Hero's single leg stance. Left leg kick.

Lift the left leg into a crane stance. Then kick out with a left leg toe kick at a 45-degree angle to the left side.

二六、猛虎出洞坐馬架打式

26 - Vicious tiger comes out of the cave.
Sit on horse stance.
Block and strike.

Place the left foot on the ground, then push off with the left foot as the right leg slides past the left so that you sit in a horse stance. As you are moving into the horse stance, the left hand blocks upward as you strike with a right vertical fist. Again, your hand stance is 45-degrees off the centerline.

二七, 合 步 連 環 拳

27 - "Bring the feet together" stance.
Continuous punch.

As you bring the left foot alongside the right foot, the left fist moves in a clockwise downward block as the right vertical fist comes out to strike. The right fist brushes past the inside of the left elbow as it comes out to strike. The left hand remains as a fist.

back view

二八. 穿 心 舞 花 十 字 拳

28 - Pierce the heart. (Hands) dancing with the flowers. "Ten" character fist.

Turn to your left and step your right foot past the front of the left foot so that you temporarily sit in a right T-stance. Bring your right arm over and down and cross both arms in front of you in an "X" position, so that the right arm is on the outside.

Then step forward with the left leg into a left bow stance and raise both fists to shoulder level. Strike outward with both arms. Look to your left side.

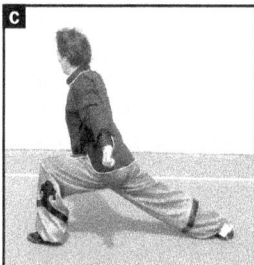

二九. 坐 馬 打 虎 式

29A - Sit on horse stance.
Strike the tiger (right).

Turn your waist slightly to the right so that you temporarily sit in a horse stance. Then make a downward sideways block with the left outer forearm, and strike with your right forearm (or fist). Simultaneously, shift into the left bow stance.

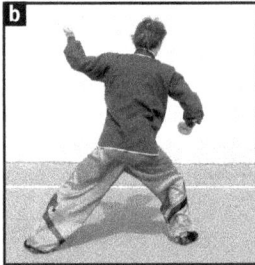

二九. 坐 馬 打 虎 式

29B - Sit on horse stance. Strike the tiger (left).

Then, make a right downward block and strike with the left outer forearm (or fist). Shift into a right bow stance.

二九. 坐 馬 打 虎 式

29C - Sit on horse stance. Strike the tiger posture

Finally, to complete the "Strike the tiger" posture, move the left hand in a clockwise circle and raise your right arm up. As your arms cross, the right arm is on the outside. Sit in a horse stance.

三十、丁步撩陰拳

30 - Uppercut to the groin, fist strike.
Left cat stance.

The left foot will step past the front of the right foot so that you sit in a left cat stance at a 45-degree angle. Strike upward with the left fist as the right fist withdraws to the right side of the body. Some will do this movement with a grabbing motion of the left hand but this is not pictured. I use a left uppercut fist strike. Either way is acceptable.

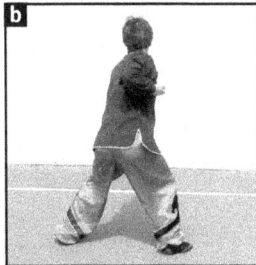

三一、回身上步坐馬架打式

31 - Reverse the body.
Step forward.
Sit on horse stance.
Block and punch.

Now bring the left foot past the front of the right foot so that you face to the other side. As you sit in a horse stance, block down and then lift upward with the left forearm and strike straight ahead with a right vertical fist.

三二. 旋風腿

32 - Tornado kick.

Lift up the left leg; push off with the right leg and do a "tornado" kick. Note that this particular tornado kick requires that you make approximately a revolution and a half circle with your entire body, so this tornado kick requires that you turn further to your left than other tornado kicks. In other words, you might need to generate a bit more torque when doing this kick. If you want to do this kick in the same manner as all the other tornado kicks, you can also simply twist your body a little more to the left after completing the tornado kick. In other words, some will attempt to turn further in the air during the kick, while others will simply handle the added distance in the turn by turning further after they have landed.

蓉 地 舞 花 金 鶏 獨 立

33 - Come down to the ground. (Hands) dancing with the flowers. Golden rooster single leg stance.

Land on your left leg and turn towards your left. You will end up facing in the opposite direction. As you stamp your right foot on the ground, push your right forearm down and bring your left forearm up. As you lift up the left leg into a crane stance, revolve both hands in a complete clockwise circular motion, with both hands making revolutions of a circle and a half. Finally, the left hand will hook outward and to the left using a crane's beak and the right palm will push outward and to the right.

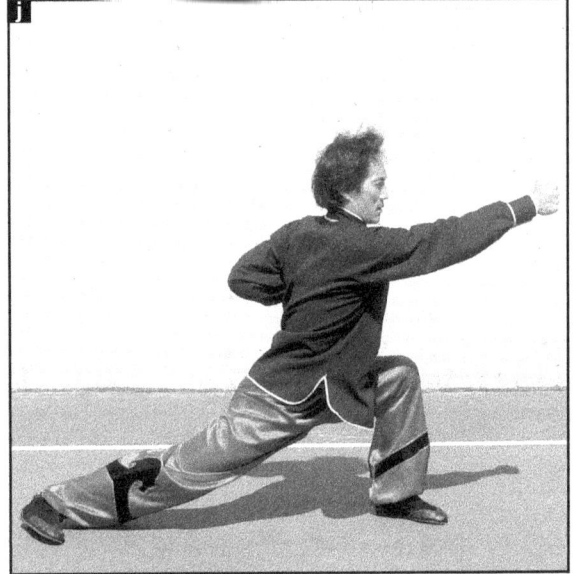

三四. 猛虎歸山搶羊勢

34 - Vicious tiger returns to the mountain. "Seize the lamb" posture.

The left foot will step down, and then the right foot will come forward behind the left foot to stamp the ground. The left foot will then step forward so that you sit in a left bow stance. While moving forward, the right hand will make a clockwise clearing/grabbing motion, followed by the same motion of the left hand. Finally, the right vertical fist will strike forward as you shift into a left bow stance.

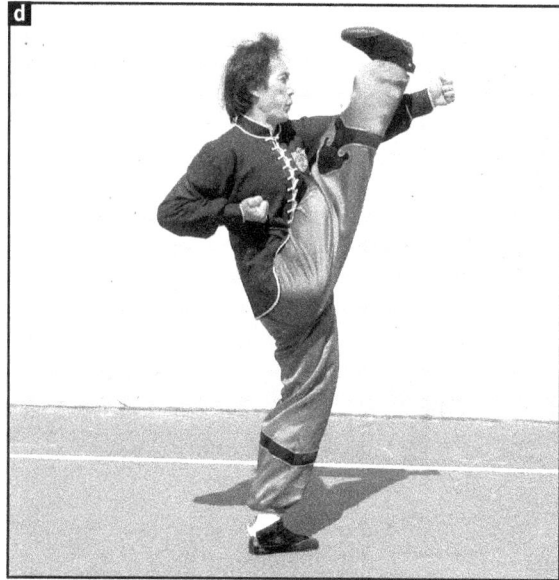

三五. 十 字 腿

35A - "Ten" character kick. Left punch.

Kick forward with the right heel and punch forward with a left vertical fist. Bring your weight forward so that your kick has power.

五．右打

35B - Right punch.

Then, while withdrawing your right leg to sit in a left bow stance, punch forward with a right vertical fist as the left hand withdraws to the left side of the body.

back view

三六、右轉左右衝拳坐馬式

36 - Turn to the right. Left, right thrusting punches. Sit on horse stance.

Turn to your right and shift into a horse stance. As you sit down in your horse stance, withdraw both left and right fists to your shoulder level. Then, punch out simultaneously to both sides of your body. Look to your right side.

三七. 迎 面

37A - Approaching the face.

Step your right leg past the left leg so that you sit in a left T-stance. The right leg will step behind the left leg as it moves to the left T-stance. Turn your body to the right and bring the left arm down to the right arm so that the outside of the left forearm rests against the inside of the right forearm. Both hands are now open.

side view

side view

三七. 舞花倒退步

37B - Dancing with the flowers. Step back.

While stepping back with the left leg into a right cat stance, both hands begin to make a large counter-clockwise motion, the left hand going up and the right hand going down. Both hands will continue their circular motion. The left palm will move upward past the bicep of the right arm while the right hand hooks downward. Finally, the left palm will face outward and the right hand will end in the crane's beak position. Notice that this is the opposite motion of this typical movement in the Northern Shaolin Style. The same applies to the hand motion of #37A.

115

三八、前摸

38A - Front sweep.

Move both hands to your left side as you sweep forward with the right leg in a counter-clockwise motion. Place both hands on the floor.

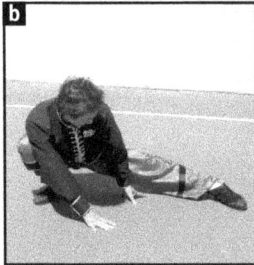

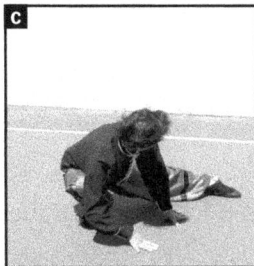

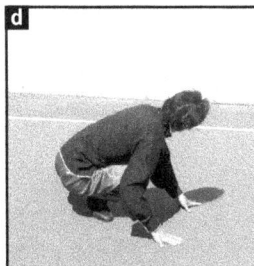

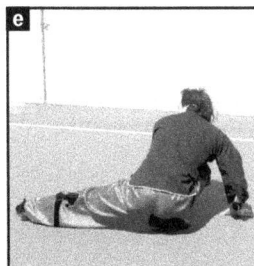

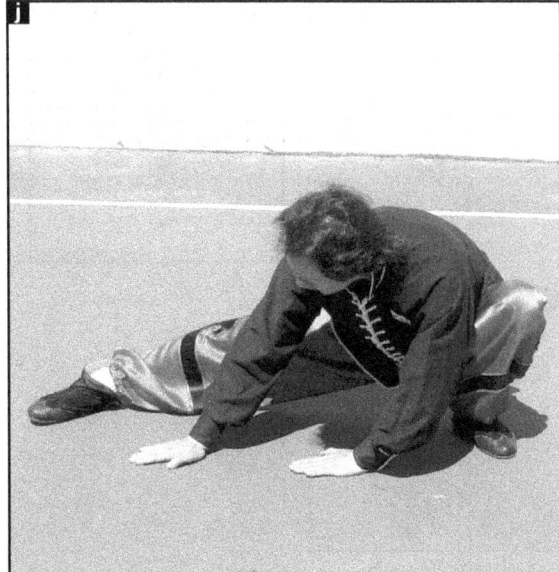

三八. 後掃拍地飛沙

38B - Back sweep.
Slap the ground.
Flying sand.

Next, shift your weight onto the right leg and while turning your body counterclockwise to the left, place your hands on the floor. You will be in a left scattered stance. Continue turning your body towards your left, and slide your left foot along the ground. The motion your left leg makes is the left back sweep. Slap the ground with both hands as you end in a left scattered stance. As with most of the sweeps of this type, rise up slightly about three-quarters of the way upon completion of the left leg sweep so that your feet switch places smoothly and so that you can slap the ground with coordinated power.

117

三九、二起腿

39 - Double kick.

Rise up, and take a step forward with the left leg and then the right leg. Then swing up the left leg, followed by the right leg so that you do the "double kick." Slap the instep of the right foot with the right palm.

side view

四十、落地左轉

40A - Come down to the ground. Turn left. Approach the face.

After completing the double kick, you will land on the left leg. Follow the body's momentum and fall forward with the right leg. Then turn to your left so that you face in the opposite direction.

The left foot will step past the right leg and you will sit in a right T-stance. Push the arms together so that the lower part of the right forearm rests on the upper part of the left forearm with the hands open. The blade edges of both palms face downward and both palms face outward.

side view

四十、舞花倒退步丁式

40B - (Hands) dancing with the flowers. Step back. Left cat stance.

While stepping back with the right leg into a left cat stance, both hands will begin to make a large clockwise motion, the right hand going up and the left hand going down. Both hands will continue their circular motion. The right palm will move upward past the bicep of the left arm while the left hand comes upward and then hooks downward. Finally, the right palm will face outward and the left hand will end in the crane's beak position.

四一、 退步穿掌

41A - Step back.
Piercing palm.

Take a step backwards with your left leg so that your right leg is at a 45-degree angle from your left leg. You will be in a right bow stance. Put the left palm at the side of the body and then thrust the right arm forward and out, palm up. Thrust the left palm forward into the right palm. The back of the left palm sits on the top of the right palm.

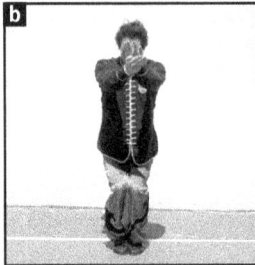

四一、收式

41B - Closing posture.

Step back and bring the right foot alongside the left foot. Bring both hands to the middle and slap the outsides of your palms against your thighs. Bring the arms all the way up.

Push down with both palms. Bow. Finally, raise your torso back to an upright position. You have now completed Shaolin #4, Pierce the Heart.

Shaolin #4: Pierce the Heart - Back Views

Shaolin #4: - Back Views

The following set of photos show the movements as back views. This is how they would appear to someone standing behind an instructor. The numbers match the front view photos given in the earlier section of the book.

 3-e
 4-a
 4-e
 5A-b

 5A-c
 5B-b
 5C-a
 5C-c

 6-b
 6-c
 6-h
 7A-a

 7A-d
 7B-a/b
 7B-c
 7B-d

 7B-g
 8A-a
 8A-b
 8A-d

8A-e

8B-b

8B-c

9A-b

9A-d

9B-c

9B-e

9C-a/b

9C-c

9C-e

9C-e/f

9C-g

10-a

10-c

11A-a

11A-b

11A-f

11B-a

11B-c

11B-c

128

 16g
 16-h
 17A-c
 17B-c

 17C-a/b
 17C-b/c
 17C-e
 18A-a

 18A-c
 18A-f
 18B-a
 18B-b

 19A-a
 19A-c
 19A-d
 19A-e

 19A-h
 19B-a
 19B-e
 20A-a

20A-b

20A-d

20A-e

20A-g

20B-a

20B-c

21A-a

21A-c

21A-d

21B-a

21B-c

21B-d

21C-a

21C-b

21C-c

21C-e

21C-g

22-b

22-d

23A-c

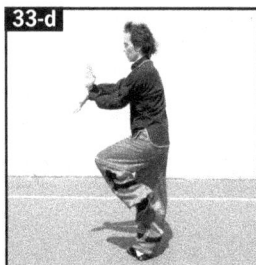

 38A-a
 38A-b
 38A-c
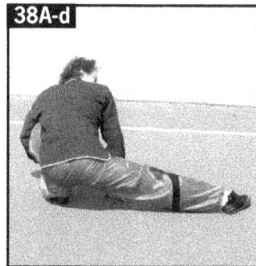 38A-d

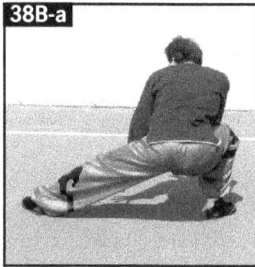 38B-a
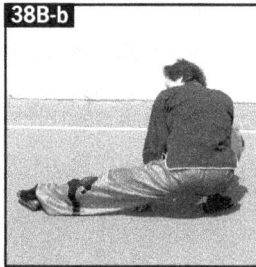 38B-b
 38B-d
 38B-e

 38B-g
 38B-h
 38B-j
 39-b

 39-c
 39-d
 39-g
 40A-b

 40A-c
 40A-d
 40A-e
 40B-a

Shaolin #4: Selected Applications

Shaolin #4: Selected Applications

As many applications have already been shown in the books on Shaolin #5, #6, #7, #8 and #1, we will not show applications for every single movement in the set. Also, be aware that there are multiple applications for every movement and there is nothing wrong with creating your own applications. Although I have my own preferences for what I believe a movement is for, I know that many people may have very different applications in mind. This is good as it allows the style to remain relevant and useful in the modern day. Adapt the set's movements in a way you think best.

Be aware that feeling and sensitivity, of a tactile nature and to the situation at hand, are extremely important. Also, be confident in your skills but never overestimate your own physical and mental capabilities.

2 - Hands dancing with the flowers. Seven stars. Shoot up to the sky like a cannon (uppercut). Left cat stance.

This move is one of the most important moves in the entire set and is the signature move of the form. Some call this the "piercing heart" move, although in actuality, this is not the name of this particular movement in the form.

As the opponent strikes with his right hand, parry it to the right side by using an upward clockwise movement of the right forearm. The right fist is held palm up. As he strikes with his left hand, parry this strike using your left forearm, also using a clockwise motion. As you close the distance, uppercut him in the throat or under the chin using the right fist. This move follows the age-old kung fu pattern of block, block, and then strike.

2 continued.

2 - Alternate.

Alternatively, you could strike him in the chest and "pierce the heart." Notice that I did use the words "pierce the heart," and that is why many would think that this movement would have that name.

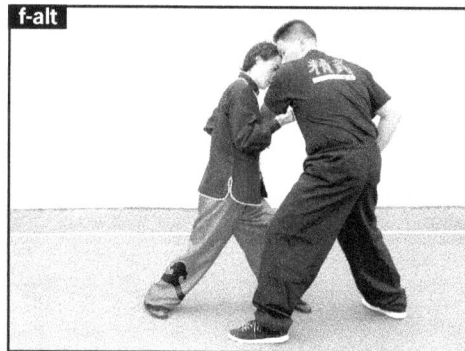

4 -   Rear coiling kick.

If you happen to be standing close to your opponent and his legs are spread, push off with your left foot and strike his groin with the bottom of your left foot. This is a surprise move and most people will not expect a kick like this. (At least in a "fair" fight they won't, but we are talking about serious self-defense situations where you must do what you need to do to survive.) Realize that this will change your relationship with your opponent in the future and if there is further discussion, the tenor of your opponent's tone will surely change.

5 - Pulling hand (left).
Straight thrust punch (right).

As he punches with his right hand, grab his right arm with your left hand and strike him in the throat with your right fist. This must be done rapidly, because if you do not strike him first, he may strike you with his free left hand. Speed is the key here. Remember that the position of your body relative to your opponent's is not always optimal and you may sometimes have to use sheer speed to keep the edge over your opponent. A strong tactile sense is also useful.

This technique works best if you grab his left arm with your left hand and then strike him with your right hand. This makes it harder for him to hit you with his opposite (right) hand since he will be impeded by his own left arm.

8A - Hammering downward thrust punch.

As your opponent punches you with his left hand, make contact with his left arm using a counterclockwise upward motion with your left arm; then pull him downward by sliding down his arm and yanking his wrist with your left hand. Finally, strike him in the neck with your right fist. Since your opponent is clearly a bully and you are acting in self-defense, you are allowed to hurt more than just his feelings.

Continued on next page.

8B - Scoop the moon's reflection from the bottom of the sea.

If he tries to punch you with his right hand, block upward with your right arm; then uppercut him beneath the chin with your left fist.

8B continued.

Alternatively, you may initiate the action by throwing a high arcing strike at his head with your right fist. He will then block your punch with his right forearm.

As he blocks your high strike, reach down to his southern region and grab him hard with your left hand. Sometimes it is said that visualization bring success, so imagine yourself not a Northern Shaolin stylist, but a dedicated Eagle Claw practitioner with decades of iron-grip training. This move will give new meaning to the song *He's Got the Whole World in His Hands*. Now sing it with me.

9A - Left hand presses down, right thrust punch.
Front heel kick.

Parry his punch downward and punch him in the face with your right hand and kick him in the stomach using your right heel. This is the "pierce the heart" kick.

9C - Turn around.
"Standing up straight" posture.

Use a clockwise swing of your right hand to parry his right hand strike. Follow the arc of your right hand with your left hand and control his right elbow momentarily with your left hand. Finally, grab the wrist of his right hand with your right hand and strike him in the face with the back of your left wrist. There are many movements in Chinese kung-fu of the type "parry, control, and strike."

10 - Lazy dragon stretches his back.
Right bow stance.

As he attempts to grab you with his left hand, parry/grab it with your left hand; then slip your right arm under his and strike him beneath the chin with the fingertips of your right hand.

11A - Steal a step. (Right) Lotus kick.

As he punches you with a right cross, step to your left and parry his blow with both hands. Bring your right leg up high in a clockwise arc and strike him in the head. It is an advantage to be able to attack him from his "blind" side.

14-15 - Vicious tiger comes out of the cave.
Sit on horse stance.
Block and strike.
"Bring the feet together" stance.
Continuous punch.

Initiate the action by faking a low right hand strike. He blocks it with his left hand and then fires off a right hand strike of his own. Parry his left hand strike downward using a clockwise block of your left hand; then punch him in the face with your right hand. In a sense you are climbing up his body with your fist strikes. This is another very common combination in kung fu.

You can also use a right backfist to his head if you so desire.

14-15 continued.

18A - Strike the bell and hit the drum.

This move is useful for the fairer sex… actually, it's useful for anyone who gets grabbed. If he grabs both of your shoulders, clap his eardrums hard with both of your hands, hence the name "Strike the bell and hit/beat the drum." Do not do this hard to someone you are simply practicing with; you may cause serious damage to their eardrums and permanently affect their ability to hear clearly.

Continued on next page.

19 -   Step forward.
       Swinging kick to the face.

Use your whirlwind arms to distract him
or block his strikes. As he attempts to block
what he sees as your low left leg kick, swing
your right leg up with force to hit him on the
side of his head.

Movements of this type also indicate that
long ago, people may have taken advantage of
the long sleeves of their robes to distract and
confuse their opponents.

19 continued.

21 - Left hand presses down, right thrust punch. Front heel kick.

This is an alternate application to the movement #9-1. Block his right hand strike with an upward motion of your left forearm. Kick him between the legs with your right foot and use great force. Remember that although Northern Shaolin stylists practice high kicks in their forms, they have the ability in self-defense situations to execute low kicks even faster and with greater ease. Also, be forewarned that if you use this move, your opponent may not speak to you in a civil manner for a long time afterwards. Please do not blame the author for your opponent's subsequent surliness. It is possible that you may lose a potential friend if you execute this move as such.

37A - Approach the face.

Block his kick using an 'X' block with both hands.

37B - Dancing with the flowers. Step back.

Hook his right punch with your right hooking hand and pull his hand to your right side.

38A - Front sweep.

Then move in low and hook his right leg with your right leg. This should cause him to lose his balance and fall if you do this move with perfect execution and timing. For a light person to sweep a heavy person, the timing is especially critical.

39 - Double kick.

Run forward and parry his punches away, down, and to the outside. Leap up and kick him in the throat. This is a very special technique and should be done with the utmost caution. Remember, flying kicks make the practitioner very vulnerable upon landing.

Names of the Movements in Shaolin #4

Names of Movements of Shaolin #4

1   Immortal shakes his clothes.
Step forward.
Double matching fists.

2   (Hands) Dancing with the flowers.
Seven Stars.
Shoot up to the sky like a cannon (uppercut).
Left cat stance.

3   Hero stands on one leg.
Pick up the left foot.

4   Rear coiling kick.

5

5A)   Pulling hand (left). Straight thrust punch (right.)
5B)   Right "cross" kick or Right "ten" character kick with a left thrusting punch.
5C)   Right thrusting punch.
Left bow stance.

6   Left, right thrusting punches.
Sit on horse stance.

7

7A)   Approach the Face.
7B)   Hands dancing with the flowers.
Step back.

8

8A)   Hammering downward thrust punch.
8B)   Scoop the moon's reflection from the bottom of the sea.

9

    9A)   Left hand presses down, right thrust punch.
                Front heel kick
    9B)   Back heel kick.
    9C)   Turn around.
                "Standing up straight" posture.

10   Lazy dragon stretches his back.
           Right bow stance.

11

    11A)   Steal a step.
               (Right) Lotus kick.
    11B)   "Ten" character fist.

12   Dancing with the flowers.
           Seven stars.
           Shoot up to the sky like a cannon (uppercut).
           Left cat stance.

13   Hero's single leg stance.
           Left leg kick.

14   Vicious tiger comes out of the cave.
           Sit on horse stance.
           Block and strike.

15   "Bring the feet together" stance.
           Continuous punch.

16   Pierce the heart.
           (Hands) dancing with the flowers.
           "Ten" character fist.

17   Sit on horse stance.
    17A)   Strike the tiger (right).
    17B)   Strike the tiger (left).
    17C)   Strike the tiger posture.

18
18A) Strike the bell and hit the drum.
(Alternate name: Double wind strikes the ears.).
18B) Come down to the ground.
"Tame the tiger" stance.

19 Step forward.
Swinging kick to the face.

20
20A) Hammering downward thrust punch.
(Alternate name: Double wind strikes the ears.).
20B) Scoop the moon's reflection from the bottom of the sea.

21
21A) Left hand presses down, right thrust punch.
Front heel kick.
21B) Back heel kick.
21C) Turn around.
"Standing up straight" posture.

22 Lazy dragon stretches his back.
Right bow stance.

23
23A) Steal a step.
(Right) Lotus kick.
23B) "Ten" character fist.

24 Dancing with the flowers.
Seven stars.
Shoot up to the sky like a cannon (uppercut).
Left cat stance.

25 Hero's single leg stance.
Left leg kick.

26   Vicious tiger comes out of the cave.
         Sit on horse stance.
         Block and strike.

27   "Bring the feet together" stance.
         Continuous punch.

28   Pierce the heart.
         (Hands) dancing with the flowers.
         "Ten" character fist.

29   Sit on horse stance
   29A) Strike the tiger (right).
   29B) Strike the tiger (left).
   29C) Strike the tiger posture.

30   Uppercut to the Groin, fist strike.
         Left cat stance.

31   Reverse the body.
         Step forward.
         Sit on horse stance.
         Block and punch.

32   Tornado kick.

33   Come down to the ground.
         (Hands) dancing with the flowers.
         Golden rooster single leg stance.

34   Vicious tiger returns to the mountain.
         "Seize the lamb" posture.

35
   35A) "Ten" character kick.
         Left punch.
   35B) Right punch.

36   Turn to the right.
          Left, right thrusting punches.
          Sit on horse stance.

37
  37A)   Approaching the face.
  37B)   Dancing with the flowers.
          Step back.

38
  38A)   Front sweep.
  38B)   Back sweep.
          Slap the ground.
          Flying sand.

39   Double kick.

40
  40A)   Come down to the ground.
          Turn left.
          Approach the face.
  40B)   (Hands) dancing with the flowers.
          Step back.
          Left cat stance.

41
  41A)   Step back.
          Piercing palm.
  41B)   Closing posture.

Notes on the Names of the Movements in Shaolin #4

Notes on the names of the movements in Shaolin #4.

Movement #2
(Hands) Dancing with the flowers. Seven Stars. Shoot up to the sky like a cannon (uppercut). Left cat stance.

Literally, the Chinese words only say "dancing flowers." Every once in a while, for clarity, I might add the words, "hands," because the motion described in this case involves the hands and not the feet.

The Chinese words also do not say "Left" cat stance. I have added the "left" for clarity. Recall that the words were written for people who already practiced the style, and therefore it was understood that it would be known which particular cat stance it was. To go even further, the Chinese words do not even say "cat." That is the English word that we most use to describe this stance. The Chinese words to describe the stance have to do with the amount of weight that is placed on the front foot, therefore this stance might be called "empty" stance. The Chinese also use the words "perpendicular" to describe this stance.

Movement #3
Hero stands on one leg. Pick up the left foot.

This is a movement that may not be practiced often, and I personally did not learn the set using this motion, but as the name is here in the Chinese lyrics, I will indicate how the set could be done with this movement. Some will use this motion to indicate a left leg knee strike, while others will follow through and do the left leg kick. This name indicates that earlier generations may have practiced this set by using a left leg knee strike or crane stance at one time. Possibly, some may have executed a high front kick here. Notice that later in the set, this motion is actually followed by a high left leg toe kick..

Movement #4
Rear coiling kick.

When I learned this set, I usually went from movement #2 to movement #4. This "rear coiling kick" could have been translated as "back hook kick" or "rear twisted kick." This kick is a very common kick in Northern Shaolin.

Movement #5

5A)   Pulling hand (left). Straight thrust punch (right).

5B)   Right "cross" kick or Right "ten" character kick with a left thrusting punch.

5C)   Right thrusting punch. Left bow stance.

For movement #5A, I added in the words "left" and "right," to write "left" pulling hand, and "right" straight thrust punch. The Chinese words only say "pulling hand, straight thrust punch." Again, a few words are added for the sake of clarity.

For movement #5B, the name is the Chinese character for "ten" which looks like a cross, then the word "character, " followed by the word for "leg." The name refers to the fact that the opposite hand and opposite leg are being used to strike, in this case, the left hand and the right leg."

Movement #8

8A)   Hammering downward thrust punch.

8B)   Scoop the moon's reflection from the bottom of the sea.

The Chinese words are actually written with the words for movement #8B first, followed by the words for #8A. The reason for this is that when the Chinese words are written this way, there is a lyrical and poetic quality to this particular order (at least, that's what I've been told!). Because of things like this in the lyrics, it is easy to see why the words themselves are more useful to people who actually practice the style. It also shows the problems that arise when direct translation without explanation is done.

Movement #9

9A)   Left hand presses down, right thrust punch. Front heel kick.

9B)   Back heel kick.

9C)   Turn around. "Standing up straight" posture.

The word order for this is actually, "Left presses down, right thrust punch, front, back, heel kick, turn around, "standing up straight" posture." I have separated the names differently so that it is easier to follow the movements of the form.

Movement #11

11A)   Steal a step. (Right) Lotus kick.

11B)   "Ten" character fist.

When one leg passes behind the other, this is known as "stealing" a step. A "lotus" kick may also be referred to as an "outside crescent" kick. Because of the position of the fists with respect to the body, this movement is known as "ten" character fist. We are again seeing the reference to the "cross" character.

Movement #13
Hero's single leg stance. Left leg kick.

Because the name of movement #13 explicitly states that there is a left leg kick, this might indicate that movement #3 refers only to a left leg knee raise, but this is only conjecture.

Movement #15
"Bring the feet together" stance. Continuous punch.

Literally, the Chinese words say "together stance," but for clarity, I changed the words to "Bring the feet together, stance." The words "continuous punch" are a reference to the fact that the right fist should strike immediately after movement #14.

Movement #16
Pierce the heart. (Hands) dancing with the flowers. "Ten" character fist.

Notice that the name, "pierce the heart" appears in this movement and not movement #2. When the fists are coming together as if to strike both sides of the opponent's body, this is the "piercing heart" movement as named in the traditional lyrics.

Movement #18
18A)   Strike the bell and hit the drum.
(Alternate name: Double wind strikes the ears).
18B)   Come down to the ground.
"Tame the tiger" stance.

The words "strike the bell and hit the drum" may perhaps be a reference to the chanting and meditation ways of the Shaolin monks, who would strike bells and hit drums and chant while the incense in the temple burned. It is also possible that the words are an allusion to the effect one would have by clapping the opponent's ears. In modern times, we might say things like, "That guy really got his bell rung," if someone was hit hard in the head. Nowadays, to describe this movement, we might simply say "jump up and clap his ears/head."

Movement #19
Step forward. Swinging kick to the face.

Notice that this movement is similar to a double kick, but slightly different. The name may be different because of execution and/or application.

Movements #20-29 are a repeat of the movements from #8-17.

Movement #37

37A) **Approaching the face.**

37B) **Dancing with the flowers. Step back.**

Notice that the words for #37 are the same as the words for movement #7. However, whereas for movement #7 the left hand hooks and the right hand flashes the palm, in movement #37 the right hand hooks and the left hand flashes the palm. So the essence of both movements is preserved by the name, however, you would have to be familiar with the set or you would do an exact repeat of movement #7. Both movement #7 and movement #37 end in the left cat stance. So the hands move differently but the feet still move the same.

Movement #40

40A) **Come down to the ground. Turn left. Approach the face.**

40B) **(Hands) dancing with the flowers. Step back. Left cat stance.**

The Chinese words here did not have the lyrics "approach the face," although this motion is in fact done in the form. This is another case that shows that the lyrics are an aid to understanding the form, but that most people could not do the form by reading the lyrics alone.

Names of the Movements in Chinese Calligraphy

四路少林拳

穿心

第四路 穿心少林拳

一、仙人彈衣上步雙對拳

二、舞花七星沖天炮左丁式

三、英雄獨立提左足

四、後盤腿

五、攬手衝拳右踢十字腿

六、左右衝拳坐馬式

七、迎面舞花倒退步

八、海底撈月插拳炮拳

九、左樓右衝拳前蹬足後蹬足反身直立式

十、懶龍伸腰蹬弓式

十一、偷步擺蓮十字拳

十二、舞花七星沖天炮左丁式

十三、英雄獨立

十四、猛虎出洞坐馬架打式

十五、合步連環拳

十六、穿心舞花十字拳

十七、坐馬打虎式

十八、鐘鼓齊鳴落地伏虎式

十九、上步掛面腿

二十、回身海底撈月插拳炮拳

二一、左樓右衝拳前蹬足後蹬足反身直立式

二二、懶龍伸腰蹬弓式

二三、偷步擺蓮十字拳

二四、舞花七星沖天炮左丁式

二五、英雄獨立

二六、猛虎出洞坐馬架打式

二七、合步連環拳

二八、穿心舞花十字拳

184

Acknowledgements

Acknowledgements

Let's trot out the usual suspects to thank again! I shall mention them all.

Master Paul Eng had me go over the words with Albert Koo so that I could get the literal meaning first. He then explained the martial meaning of each of the words and mentioned that over time, the sets will change because of the variation in instructors and students. He wrote the words down, and then, Mrs. Hsiu Fong Hao, wife of Mr. Tien Shou Hao, rewrote the calligraphy clearly, so that practitioners might reference it in the future.

Phillip Wong then took the photos, many photos, many, many photos, and to some people who asked, the answer is, "No, we did not have a movie camera, but I wish we had one." I should mention that a guy gets a little tired from jumping around all day. Then we brought in Ray Woo, all the way from the Excelsior District in San Francisco. Folks, he IS that big! No camera tricks there. He did admit to me what his weight was, and even I was surprised. For fellas this big, foot sweeps don't work that well. Actually, neither do punches, kicks, etc. etc. Thanks for the big help, Big Ray. We'll nominate him for an Academy Award for his performance.

I'd also like to than Mr. John Groschwitz, M.A. in East Asian Studies, for translating the writing of Song Yuwen. As always, his translation skills are a great addition to this book.

Sifu Remus Barraca, known as "Master Killer," helped with the weapons applications. All I can say is, "I'm lucky I didn't get hurt." I need to complete this series.

Another great addition to the book was Master Paul Tam, one of the last of the old-timers with a real connection to the past. He is a gentleman in every sense of the word, and I'm honored to have spent time with him. I communicated with Master Tam by way of his student, Sifu John Wong, a high-level exponent of the art of Master Tam. If health means wealth, these guys are rich, and I want their money, or their health!

And the person who put me into contact with Master Tam and his student, Sifu John Wong, was none other than my Northern Shaolin brother, Scott Chen. Or as he told me, "My name is Chen, Scott Chen." He's as good on the dance floor as he is on the kung fu floor. He told me he was spinning, gliding, bobbing, weaving… I wasn't sure whether he was talking about Chinese boxing or dancing. Well, he showed me, that's for sure. Great Scott! I almost forgot. Thanks, Scott!

To make sure the words flow nicely for the casual reader, or even for the meticulous reader, we had the work edited by Brennan Pelosi. I'm glad we put his journalism degree to some use.

Jeffrey L. Wing, DDS, also helped with some more proofreading. Three things, number one, he is related to me, number two, we joined on the same day, and number three, *he* is the doctor!

Finally, we drag in the infamous Bruce Hopkins to forge it into book form, and voila, presto, out it comes! We keep him hopping. Click, then drag, is his mantra. I asked him what he did to complete this work. His answer was, "It's a drag, a complete drag." I hope he understood me.

Thanks for the help everyone. I think we did it again.

www.ingramcontent.com/pod-product-compliance
Lightning Source LLC
Chambersburg PA
CBHW080503110426
42742CB00017B/2979